Ms. Thang's Guide to Fly

Aine A. Thang

Yeva Press

If you purchased this book without a cover, you should be aware that it may be stolen property. It was reported as "unsold and destroyed" to the publisher and neither the author nor the publisher has received any payment for this "stripped book."

Copyright © 2002 Yeva Corporation

All rights reserved. No part of this book may be reproduced, stored in a retrieval system, or transmitted by any means, electronic, mechanical, photocopying, recording, or otherwise, without the prior written permission of the publisher. No liability is assumed with respect to damages resulting from the use of information contained herein.

Yeva Press is an imprint of:
Yeva Corporation
8362 Tamarack Village
Suite 119-284P
St. Paul, MN 55125
Visit out web site at http://yeva.com

Printed in the United States of America

ISBN 1-930758-31-6
Library of Congress Control Number 2001087814

To the fly divas of this generation puttin' it right for the ones that come after. May you find yo' Spencer and the Promised Land.

Aine A. Thang, Granny Fly

Contents

Foreword..III

Ms. Thang Speaks: Havin' My Say..............................1
Ten Ways to Tell if You a Hoochie....................................5
Top Ten Hoochie Phrases..7

Ms. Thang Speaks: Original Fly..............................10
Top Ten Hoochie Hangouts..15
Top Ten Things People Say to Hoochies..........................18

Ms. Thang Speaks: Ms. Thang's Good Thing................22
Ms. Thang's Shakin' and Bakin' Recipe............................25
Miss Fly...26
Miss Hoochie...28

Ms. Thang Speaks: Disciplines of Fly........................40
The Disciplines of Fly..45

Ms. Thang Speaks: Attractin' Spencers......................48
Eleven Quick Ways to Spot a Busta................................48
Ten Ways to Spot a Spencer..53

Ms. Thang Speaks: As Fly As You Wanna' Be ... 60
Five Signs that You Profilin' Desperation ... 63

Ms. Thang Speaks: Leave It Alone ... 68
Ten Reasons Why Bein' a Hoochie Hurt You ... 71

Ms. Thang Speaks: Or Get It Together ... 78
The Hoochie Makeover ... 78
Dream Crazy ... 80
A Life of Legacy ... 83
Top Ten Fly Divas ... 86

Ms. Thang Speaks: On Purpose Fly ... 94
Top Ten Hoochie Career Opportunities ... 98
Ms. Thang's Road Map to Purpose ... 103
Ms. Thang's Top Nine Purpose Issues ... 117

Ms. Thang Speaks: 360-Degree Fly ... 133
120 Degrees—Money-wise ... 133
120 Degrees—Body-wise Fly ... 137
120 Degrees—Spirit-wise Fly ... 139

Ms. Thang Speaks: The Nature of Fly ... 144
Appendix ... 151
Ms. Thang Terminology Guide ... 152

Foreword

A man, living in a country where polygamy is an accepted way of life, can choose to marry as many women as he wishes. He marries a beautiful, voluptuous woman trained in the arts of pleasure, with nothing in her head but the desire to please.

He marries again; she, also, is a beautiful, voluptuous woman trained in the arts of pleasure. In addition to her beauty, however, this wife has a great deal of cleverness. Her husband finds that he can come to her to talk about problems and to get advice or, perhaps, simply for the pleasure of her company. She has a great sense of humor and a mind for management. She has made the effort to develop in all areas of her being: her mind, her body, and her spirit.

Which wife should the man favor?

Your answer to that question reveals a lot about your own mindset—and your attitude about enhancing yourself as a woman.

Despite burning our bras and declaring our freedom, American women seem to have lost the way along the path to women's rights. We desire our relationships with men to be equal. We desire love and understanding. Yet, the freedom for which we've fought so long has left far too many of us with nothing but burnt bras and failed symbolism.

Rather than delivering us to the fairness of equal pay for equal work, increased opportunities for women to lead, and equal responsibility in our relationships with men, the legacy of feminism is a mixed bag of gains and losses. On one hand, women are graduating from college in higher numbers than are men; on the other, many women still feel the need to use their bodies, rather than their minds, to get ahead in this world.

Consider this: Our country leads the world in the number of teenage pregnancies.

Why?

I believe that part of the answer lies in a basic misinterpretation of feminism. Somewhere along the way, feminism became more about sexual freedom than talent and ability. When that happened, the legacy of feminism was weakened.

Moreover, feminism disregarded our sons and thereby created a backlash that reverberates in our daughters' lives. Want proof? While the United States leads in the number of teenage pregnancies, there is no corresponding growth in responsibility on the male side of the equation. And why should there be? After all, the message of misdirected feminism is that women can do it all.

But do we want to? And, more importantly, where are the answers to the problems created by our misdirection?

Although many would revile the aged of our communities, I often find solace in talking to my grandmother, Ms. Thang. She has lived through wars, the Civil Rights Movement, the assassination of a president and the death of his golden child, the assassination of Martin Luther King, Jr., and Malcolm X, the death of apartheid, as well as a great deal of technological advancement.

Searching for answers in response to being insulted for my view on propriety, I posed the question of "Which woman should the man favor?" to grandmother. Her response was expansive. What follows is a summation, in her words and her rather . . . well, ethnic patois. Nevertheless, her words are for all people in this country.

One final note: Those of us who are of African American descent are surely aware that the African American culture is a culture of three voices.

Voice One is the voice of the privileged and the educated. Either they were born to privilege, or they have worked hard and have seized the advantages available to them. They have taken hold of freedom's bounty and live lives to the fullest of their purpose and potential.

Voice Two is the voice of those in the middle. This voice is typical of most of us. It is a voice of striving and achieving. It is a Pioneer voice. Those who speak with this voice know first-hand of forging a way and walking in little-traveled paths. This is the fluid voice of the American dream. It is multi-dialectic, skipping agilely from cultural speech patterns to more standardized patterns, making that transition in accordance with the situation at hand.

Voice Three is the voice of the uneducated. Those who speak with this voice may not have had access to the best educational system. Maybe they dropped out of school, or maybe they grew up during a time when education wasn't considered as important as having a job. Sometimes, an uneducated voice can reflect an age in which educational opportunities were limited by race or circumstance.

Whatever the case, the distinctions matter little. All that matters is that these are the three voices of my culture and, truly, of my nation. I caution you, reader, to understand that these voices of an American culture are often a matter of economic reality, rather than racial reality.

Yet, more than economics, the three voices carry the tonality of origin, history, hope, and cultural pride.

To the uninitiated and the arrogant, the third voice of my community might seem an insulting dialect to employ when speaking to a diverse audience, but those who speak in the dialects of this very diverse culture know that to know these words makes you a part of a vital COMMUNITY linked by a history of courage.

Those who speak the voice of the educated and the uneducated understand that respect is due all three voices. The Voices are at once Poetic, fluid, and historical. These are the voices of my people. The words are an oral history of my people. And, when one takes the time to listen, wisdom can be found within the timbre of each voice.

And that third voice, that uneducated voice, can speak words that bind us together in what Granny Fly calls the COMMUNITY.

Moreover, while my grandmother speaks with the third Voice, her strivings have birthed two generations of educated voices.

Those of use who are her progeny are greatly indebted to

her. We love her and respect her role as matriarch.

As my grandmother would say, 'Ms. Thang knows what she's talking about!'

In peace,

Miss Sidditty

Ms. Thang Speaks

Havin' My Say

CHAPTER 1
▼
Havin' My Say

I been waitin' for years to have my say. Thought I was goin' to have to get as old as them Delaney girls, and I'd do it, too, but my time is now.

Alright, now! It's 'bout time somebody took a minute to back up and listen. Ain't no thing I can talk to more than women and they men. And fly, flava, jiggy, all of 'em jest the same sauce in a different package. They all mean the same thing.

A lot of young girls these days so desperate for some notice, they tradin' down smooth for I-don't know-what, but I hear 'em callin' it FLY.

Hmph! Don't know much, but I know fly. And believe you me, fly don't mean wearin' hemlines as necklines. Fly don't mean mean hangin' out an open-for-business-24/7 sign 'round yo' neck.

That ain't nowhere close to fly. Back in the day, we used ta' call girls ain't got no mo' sense than to show all they got, *hoochie mamas*; these days, they jest callin' 'em hoochies.

Aine A. Thang

'Course, back in my day, girls dressin' in nothin' but nothin' didn't get no million-dollar contracts sellin' soda water neither. Times sure has changed, and they ain't changed for the better.

Now, Lord bless me, I might got one foot in the Hallelujah and another on a slippery slope, but I ain't gone yet. As long as I got the floor, I intend on speakin' my mind. My granddaughter, Ms. Sidditty, she get offended easy. She what they call "politically correct." Well, that's all fine and good, but when you as close to seein' yo' maker as I am, you find yo'self more concerned with tellin' the truth 'bout things.

And the truth is, I don't see no reason to stand here an' lie 'bout what to call you if you livin' like a hoochie. Girl, if you livin' like one, then you are one. Ain't no reason to try an' glue the bark back on the tree after you done tore it off.

I'm old and, Lord knows, I'm tired. Ain't got time to figure out how to please nobody but myself. 'Sides, the glory of bein' old is bein' able to tell it like it is.

You young'uns, you keep on bein' correct, that's what you got in yo' life, but Ms. Thang got ta' break it down right.

See, Ms. Thang a *fly-losopher*. My life callin' is to drop knowledge on fly. C'mon now. Ms. Thang don't play when it come to the science of fly. I'm in the club, ya'll. That there is why I got the goods on fly. 'Sides that, I got plenty of time on my hands. Don't like knittin' for folks that won't wear what I make, so I watch TV. It helps me keep up with what's goin' on in the world. Truth to tell, seein' what's goin' on in the world give me a real sense of peace 'bout goin' to the hereafter. Don't look for

Ms. Thang's Guide to Fly

Ms. Thang to miss none of y'all. Folks downright crazy these days.

Uh huh.

Crazy ain't my topic though, so I'll leave that alone, maybe hit it in my next book.

Now, I know folks don't like to hear a lot of jawin' and preachin'. They want good advice packed up like a thirty-second commercial. So, to make Ms. Thang's little bit quick and easy, my granddaughter and I put most of what I got to say in a bunch of top-ten lists.

Since I don't know much 'bout all this feminism stuff she wanna' talk 'bout, I ain't hittin' on nothin' like. My words got to do with gainin' ground in life and bein' with the right man. The rest of it you got to figure out for yo'self.

Jest so ya'll know, Ms. Thang been on both sides of the fence. I been on the side where I didn't want nobody's good advice, which led me to the *Consequences* side. From the *Consequences* side I made it through to the Promised Land. For me, the Promised Land meant that I worked doin' what I wanted. I met me a good man. We was married for 30 years before he went on to Glory. We was partners, lovers, and good friends.

Me and Spencer built us a good life. We raised children, had granbabies; we shared our lives and our loads. I was blessed to have Spencer in my life, but before I met him, I learned a few things on the *Consequences* side. I also learned from Spencer. I passed that knowledge down to my own four children. And Ms. Thang got her mind set to share those lessons with you.

Right now, I got a word or two 'bout findin' a Spencer. First off, Spencers ain't hangin' 'round down at the mall talkin' smack. And more important, Spencers ain't lookin' for the kind of fly that only go skin deep.

I got me two boys of my own, and back when they was young I started speakin' to them 'bout stayin' away from hoochies. Ain't nothin' worse for a man lookin' to be somebody than a hoochie. Hoochies don't jest mess up they own lives, they crashin' and burnin' ev'rybody they touch.

I been waitin' for years to have my say. Thought I was goin' to have to get as old as them Delaney girls, and I'd do it, too, but my time is now.

So, watch out, all you little hoochies thinkin' you fly, 'cause the original fly diva, Ms. Thang, is 'bout to have her say.

Ms. Thang's Guide to Fly

(Let's get this party started off right.)

Ten Ways to Tell if You a Hoochie*

1. Girl, you know you a Hoochie if you got kids and couldn't say who they daddy was if a winnin' lottery ticket depended on it.

2. Girl, you know you a Hoochie if you show up on Jenny Jones or Montel Williams tryin' to get a paternity test for three or four of yo' current boyfriends.

3. Girl, you know you a Hoochie if you afraid yo' family wouldn't recognize you without them fake nails, fake hair, fake boobs, fake rear, fake lashes, fake jewelry, fake sex-kitten accent, and all that other fake stuff you wearin' right now.

4. Girl, you know you a Hoochie if you put on a bra and folks don't know you.

5. Girl, you know you a Hoochie if the cosmetics companies come knockin' on yo' door offerin' you free membership in they customer loyalty program for people-who-put-on-they-makeup-with-a-shovel.

Aine A. Thang

6. Girl, you know you a Hoochie if you keep gettin' calls from strangers tellin' you they saw yo' ad on the wall in the men's room.

7. Girl, you know you a Hoochie if folks think yo' name is Shake-It-But-Don't-Break-It-Cause-The-Trashman-Won't-Even-Take-It.

8. Girl, you know you a Hoochie if Tyrique pay yo' rent, Michael pay yo' bills, and Anthony buy yo' groceries.

9. Girl, you know you a Hoochie if you ain't care how much silicone leak, you keepin' them fake up-frontahs.

10. Girl, you know you a Hoochie if you have a standin' contract with all the talk shows sayin' that you willin' to come on they show anytime, wearin' next-to-nothin', and talkin' trash to the audience.

(This is all in fun. If you find yo'self gettin' too offended, you might want to call "Hoochies Anonymous." They can help.)

Ms. Thang's Guide to Fly

(Still ain't sure whether you hoochie or fly? Check yo' words.)

Top Ten Hoochie Phrases

1. Baby, you so fine. Can't nobody even tell you nigh-on-to ninety-five. By the way, baby, you don't think yo' kids and four ex-wives will try to contest that new Will you made up, do you?

2. You know you want a piece of this. (Said while slappin' yo' rear end.)

3. I'm all that. (Said to sneerin' audience members durin' Hoochie talk shows.)

4. I don't care how many men I slept with. You that baby's father!

5. You jest jealous 'cause you ain't got none of these. (Said while pushin' yo' silicone breasts together.)

6. Naw, girl, these thangs ain't real. They silicone. They an investment in my future.

7. I know you paid for dinner, but I got other bills, too.

8. Uh, the reason yo' friend was sittin' buck-naked on my bed was that he was. . . he was checkin' out the mattress springs to make sure they worked. You know you been complainin' 'bout that squeaky sound. I jest wanted it to be a surprise for you, baby.

9. I got a clean bill of health on my blood test. (Say this while crossin' yo' fingers behind yo' back.)

10. I said, ain't nothin' goin' on, 'til my rent get paid, you got that?

CANE SENSE

These days I need the help of a cane to get me to places I need to go. That cane of mine got many a use, too, like knockin' sense into folks can't hear nothin' but what they want to hear. I know that ain't you so don't be actin' crazy. Mick ears, girl, this knowledge I'm droppin' for free. If you smart, you will learn from the cane without the pain. Check out cane sense for good sense all condensed.

Girl, folks done got so confused these days. They flipped the script callin' the hoochie look fly an' the fly look flat. Ms. Thang here to set that wrong to right.

Girl, wearin' yo' hemline 'round yo' neck ain't nowhere near fly.

Ms. Thang Speaks

Original Fly

CHAPTER 2
▼
Original Fly

The first step in bein' fly all 'bout discipline. Has to be. 'cause findin' yo' way in life take work. That there's somethin' you need to know from the git go.

While you scopin' what Ms. Thang got to say 'bout the hoochie life, you got to realize that one of the main differences between hoochie and fly is that hoochies spend they time makin' excuses 'bout the whys an' the wherefores. You know what I'm sayin'? Hoochies bankin' on they looks, thinkin' that's how they gonna' get over.

Now I ain't tryin' to say a body can't get by on they looks. They can. Told you I spend most of my time watchin' the television. 'Bout all a body see on TV is folks gettin' by on they looks.

Ms. Thang brangin' the noise, now. I'm tellin' the truth. Long as you listenin' to the truth, you ought ta' know that true fly ain't got nothin' to do with what you look like. Fly got ev'rythin' to do with attitude.

Attitude.

Girl, if you want to get fly and stay fly, then you got to

cultivate the fly attitude.

Perk up, now, 'cause Ms. Thang 'bout to break off a little som'in, som'in for ya'll.

See, the first step in bein' fly all 'bout discipline. Has to be. 'Cause findin' yo' way in life take work. That there's somethin' you need to know from the get go.

Gettin' fly take dreamin' and plannin' and doin'.

Sometime it mean gettin' the door slammed in yo' face, and movin' on to the next door. It take seein' some dreams die, while other dreams live.

But, most of all, fly take discipline.

All right, Ms. Thang droppin' science now. Ya'll listen up 'cause this here a black grandma talkin'—make that a black grandma diva, loud mike. I said discipline is the key to what Ms. Nikki G. call "transformation and redemption."

Ms. Nikki talkin' to Black folks, but it seem to me that the words got health to a lot of folk.

I ain't aimin' to say I know all 'bout what Ms. Nikki is preachin' and teachin', but Ms. Girl been writin' for a while now. I think she got somethin' worth leanin' an ear to.

Some of you wannabe fly chicks out there playin' hoochie-hoo, ya'll need to quit playin' and transform yo'selves.

I ain't talkin' 'bout the flava'-o'-the-month fashion statement. I ain't talkin' 'bout brushin' on a coat of paint and callin' yo'self transformed. Ms. Thang talkin' 'bout transformation back to original fly. Come on now, true fly ain't got nothin' to do with how much makeup you wearin'. Fly a spectrum of color and looks, girl. Ms. Fly come exotic, plain,

Ms. Thang's Guide to Fly

and ev'ry kind of look in between. That's 'cause fly is 'bout a mindset. It's 'bout how you see yo'self and others.

Don't tell me I don't know what I'm talkin' 'bout. Ms. Thang a card-carryin' member of the Fly club. Ain't nowhere mentioned in the bylaws I been readin' that fly mean you got to wear hot pants that look like underpants.

Advertisin' yo' wares jest fass and nasty. And, truth to tell, fass and nasty go agin' the fly bylaws.

No need for drama, now. I'm speakin' true. Ms. Thang old enough, I invented fly. An' even if I didn't invent it myself, Ms. Thang the keeper of the flame, so sit a spell in my classroom if you wanna' know fly, 'cause, little Ms. Potentiality, that's what I'm teachin'.

Awright?

Get yo' Mickey ears on, girl. This here is grown-folk knowledge.

You hear me? Grown women do not walk 'round tryin' to advertise they wares like some kind of travelin' flea market.

You wanna' be fly?

Then you got to get this.

Ms. Nikki talkin' 'bout fly in that book of hers—*Racism 101*, she call it. Ain't nown where did she say nothin' 'bout lookin' like no fass-track hoochie.

Ms. Nikki preachin' 'bout true fly. She talkin' 'bout Community Fly. Community Fly a Black-folk thang goin' back to the day when nobody thought Black was beautiful—nobody but our own mamas and daddies, that is. Community fly started with the mind and worked its way to potential. Community fly supported our Black women, tellin' them they was smart and capable and goin' somewhere with they lives.

Comin' from slavery times, we'd done had all we could stand of bein' nothin' but willin' bodies to work and slave and put out.

Our mammas and daddies preachin' to us 'bout usin' our minds, freein' our hearts, and achievin', in spite of fear, in spite of prejudice.

Bein' fly 'bout spreadin' them dark wings and takin' to the sky.

Ain't no "booty call" in original fly.

That there Thug Fly—hard-core, hard-livin', lazy fly.

Listen up, and don't be rollin' yo' eyes. I got to tell it like it is and like it should be. I'm old and tired, too tired to put it five different ways so ain't nobody upset. I done went through too much to be old, I deserve my say. Lord have mercy.

'Sides, Ms. Thang tryin' to help somebody.

Ms. Thang tryin' to save somebody some pain an' aggravation.

Glory to God, glory to God, I jest can't see how all our strivin' and marchin' and shoutin' and dyin' in the street come to a generation of women got mo' opportunity than they know what to do with, and all a lot of 'em doin' is bein' fass and nasty.

Somebody please tell me how fass and nasty come to mean fly?

That's slave thinkin'. A lot of folk—Black, White, Brown, and green-polka-dotted-with-yella-stripes—indulgin' theyselves

Ms. Thang's Guide to Fly

in slave thinkin' and got the nerve to call it hot.

Hmph! Folk, need to ask somebody. Ya'll ain't hot. Ya'll don't know hot.

This a generation love retro. You retro-lovin' chillas need to love yo'self some retro-hot. 'Course, retro-hot also called class.

I'm tryin' to teach somebody somethin'. C'mon, work with me. You know what I'm talkin' 'bout. I know you do. Hot a lot mo' than dressin' like you can't stand the feel of thread on yo' body.

Girl, listen up and hear me right. I'll tell you hot. Hot go with red and make a sauce. Fass and nasty mo' along the lines of stinky cheese, ain't go with nothin', 'ceptin' losers an' playas and chitlins'. I guess 'cause fass and nasty full of the same thang as chitilins. You jest got Ms. Thang's final word on that subject.

You don't think bein' a hoochie nasty?

Peek my next list.

A i n e A. T h a n g

Top Ten Hoochie Hang Outs

1. Corner bar

2. Butt-to-wall in the men's bathroom

3. Sidewalk, waitin' for customers.

4. Back seat of a steamed up car

5. Police station

6. Castin' couch of a B-movie movie producer

7. Crack house

8. Talk-show green room for the you-a-loser show

9. Drug parties

10. Nowhere

Where you whilin yo' time, Ms. Got-It-Goin'-On?

Ms. Fly ain't hangin' out in holes on the off-chance she gonna' meet Mr. Right.

C'mon now, I. Quella. You smart. This here book 'bout bein' fly and attractin' fly. I'm here to tell you, you wanna

Ms. Thang's Guide to Fly

attract fly? You wanna' find a good man? Then, girl, you got to get in Spencer's way.

Somebody need to set an alligator on them words, put it in a song. Matter of fact, I'm gonna' chirp me a few bars, make myself a little refrain: Girl, in the name of fly love, get in the boy's way.

Be where he at.

That's bank knowledge, girl. I'm tellin' you straight: the only way to get a good man is to be on the path that a good man walk.

Cash them words in, or ignore 'em, your choice.

See, Spencer ain't hangin' with the rabble. He in bookstores and libraries. He shoppin' uptown. He livin' uptown, got an uptown mindset.

It's hard enough findin' Mr. Right when you lookin' in the places that Mr. Right go. Will somebody please tell me how you plan to find Mr. Right if you lookin' in places filled with Mr. Wrongs?

You can't.

Fly girls know that. They comin' out of college with MRS-degrees. They hookin' an' cookin' they big catch while hoochies cryin' they stories to the talk-show hosts.

All Ms. Thang got to say 'bout them crocodile tears is, whatever.

Get yo' own hankie while you cryin' yo' river an' chasin' five-an'-dime glory. You know what I'm sayin'? Hoochies five and dime cause they ain't willin' to put in the effort to be truly fly. Girl, if fifteen minutes of spotlight all you need from life, then my list of where to hang yo' hankie is all good.

You hangin' out where the hoochies hang and you can be a guest on the next Girl-Why-You-Thinkin'-Like-A-Fool talk show. You work it hard enough, the producer will call you.

Ain't tryin' to be hard, I'm jest speakin' gospel.

How many times you read 'bout somebody gettin' arrested off the corner, or at a drug party? How many people you heard of gettin' kilt 'cause they in the wrong place—don't matter what time.

You heard 'bout 'em, didn't you? So, I guess they got they glory, but like I say befo', that's five-an'-dime glory.

It's one way to get some fame. May not be a good way, but it is a way.

Check yo'self, girl.

Got to get yo' name in print, huh?

If it don't matter how, then you jest might be a hoochie, a desperate one, at that.

Be smart 'bout gettin yo' face known. Ain't too many folks can live down a bad reputation that they earned for theyselves, and you don't need the kind of mess that can come from bein' dumb 'bout the media.

If you want 15 minutes of fame and an eternity of pain, follow the hoochie path. If you want that 15 minutes to last a lifetime and more, do somethin' worth writin' 'bout. Do somethin' worth talkin' 'bout. Bring somethin' good out of yo'self, somethin' that folks can point to and say, "Now that's how it's done."

Makin' the world a better place, that's original fly.

Ms. Thang's Guide to Fly

(Awright, Ms. Thang got another list for you.)

Top Ten Things People Say to Hoochies

1. I'm sorry, but the paternity test show he is NOT yo' baby's father.

2. Girl, you need to put a halt on all that jigglin', else I'm afraid you gonna' get brain damage.

3. Girl, please, you ain't all that.

4. You better keep yo' hands off my man. He told you he ain't interested.

5. Sorry, we ain't hirin'.

6. Excuse me? I thought I heard you say you want a raise. (Laughs loudly.) You'll have to take that up with Mr. Jerk Boss next time you meet him at the Cockroach Motel. I'm not authorized to give merit raises based on the services YOU provide.

7. No, thank you. I'm happily married.

8. Why you wanna go talkin' 'bout commitment for, woman? Let's jest have a good time.

9. No, you didn't have yo' nasty Hoochie girlfriend up in my house. Now I'm goin' to have to fumigate.

10. Girl, what you tryin' to pretend for? You know you a hoochie. Yo' mama know it. Yo' daddy know it. And that man comin' out the bathroom with yo' phone number scribbled on his hand know it.

Ms. Thang's Guide to Fly

CANE SENSE

- Fass and Nasty ain't got no part in original fly.

- Original fly come out of the COMMUNITY and got to do with potential of the heart and the mind.

- Whether you fly or hoochie got to do with how and where you whilin' yo' time.

Ms. Thang Speaks

Ms. Thang's Good Thing

CHAPTER 3
▼
Ms. Thang's Good Thing

Good sex ain't a five-minute jog in the back seat of a car.

That last list was to-the-bone hard. But the thang you got ta' know 'bout bein' a hoochie is that people ain't thinkin' 'bout treatin' you right, 'specially not if you tellin' 'em by the way you present yo'self that you ain't got nothin' goin' on but the body God gave you.

An' please don't expect Ms Thang to feel all sorry for you. Ev'rybody I know has had theyselves hard times. Life is hard. If you ain't learned that lesson yet, you ain't 'bout to learn it from me. Unfortunately, life is harder on Hoochies than on other folks.

It's Hoochies who can't get good jobs—we ain't talkin' 'bout Hollywood or Las Vegas, now. I'm livin' in the real world.

It's Hoochies who get hurt when they realize they want commitment and can't find none, 'cause they got a reputation.

It's Hoochies who need somebody tellin 'em to wake up. You hear me? Wake up, girl.

Aine A. Thang

Ms. Thang know God don't like ugly, so don't think I'm lookin' to judge. I ain't lookin' to judge nobody. I'm lookin' to help somebody. Ya'll know a repentant Hoochie is the worst kind. And what I got to say comes from what I learned durin' my days on the *Consequences* side of the fence.

'Course, that was long ago, and I am tryin' to get into Glory now; but don't let my motives stop you from listenin'. The information still good. I guess what I'm tryin' to say is this: If you want to change yo' life, if you want better for yo'self, then listen up, 'cause Ms. Thang got somethin' to say.

I'm tryin' my best to get ya'll to see that a Hoochie lifestyle ain't healthy. Now, I ain't tryin' to convince nobody that sex is bad, so don't be callin' me outta' my name. This old head of mine smart enough to know that God created sex to be a good thing.

That's why they call it makin' love. When you makin' love, you doin' somethin' good, sharin' yo' spirit with another. That's what God created. God made it good but, glory, folks tryin' hard to mess it up!

When you ain't sharin' sex with the one you love, you jest havin' sex, or, like the young folk say, you doin' the nasty. Doin' the vonce, what they called it back in my day.

Folks these days treat sex like somethin' dirty or funny. Ain't nobody seein' it the way sex meant to be seen.

Good sex ain't a five-minute jog in the back seat of a car.

It ain't creepin' with yo' neighbor while his wife gone to work.

Lord have mercy, help me out, now.

Ms. Thang's Guide to Fly

Mick ears, girl. My Momma raised me. All the while I was growin' up, she kept her words steady runnin' round in my head. "Don't be taken in them Oxfords' deep sugar, girl," she used to say. "They some good men in the world. You ain't got to be taken in by a bad one. But, you got the choice of bein' worth they time or bein' no 'count."

No 'count 'bout the same as a hoochie to a lot of folks' way of thinkin'.

Why?

'Cause women that'll buy any line these playas feed to 'em, like they some starvin' chile from India, can't help but come 'cross desperate.

They desperate an' it show.

Jazz peeps used to call the desperate types "wolverines." Got yellow eyes steady searchin' for victims, and they claws out grabbin' at whatever get too close. Ya'll know who I'm talkin' 'bout. Women waitin' for some fool to come along ain't got the good sense ta' step out of the rain.

Girl, don't be like that. That ain't what God meant for you to have with love and sex. God want you to have it good all the way home. This ain't no cookbook, but Ms. Thang got the right recipe for the best kinda good sex. This recipe was tested for 30 years, so I know it works.

Aine A. Thang

Ms. Thang's Shakin' and Bakin' Recipe

Step One:

Two consentin' adults bein' faithful to each other. Faithfulness is important 'cause you don't want nobody bringin' home somethin' you didn't give him. I'm sure he feel the same way. Beyond that, if you know he faithful, you'll have a kind of trust that you wouldn't have if yo' man is rippin' and runnin' up the streets all the time, actin' buck wild with only-God-knows-who. (By the way, tryin' to be faithful with a few slip-ups here and there ain't good enough.)

Step Two:

Both consentin' adults need to be prepared to handle the *Consequences*. Some folk call that bein' responsible for yo' choices and actions.

Step Three:

It's alright to add a little freaky, but don't do nothin' that make you feel bad or disrespected.

Step Four:

Add love and respect and commitment, 'else you crossin' that line from fly to hoochie.

Ms. Thang's Guide to Fly

Now that you got my recipe, cook it right. I ain't give out that recipe so you can funk it up. You got to follow the directions on the package.

I done had my say 'bout bein' a hoochie. So I guess it's time to look at how fly style and hoochie style different.

First off, whether you Ms. Fly or Miss Hoochie depend on yo' attitude. That's a given. Get that attitude right, girl, then, like the sister says, "Step Out with Style." Here go my list of ten ways to tell if you fly...or not.

Ms. Fly Self-image

1. Fly draw attention to yo' style, not jest yo' body.

2. Fly style show USS—Unique Self Style.

3. Fly style send a message 'bout how you see yo' own value.

4. Fly style let you accentuate yo' beauty, without makin' other people feel bad.

Aine A. Thang

Promotin' Yo'self

    5. Fly style let you be seen with the all movers an' shakers—and not get put on the throw-away list.

    6. Fly style let you make yo' own opportunity.

    7. Fly style work for you, helpin' you earn what you worth.

Ms. Fly Relationships

    8. Fly style make winners take you seriously.

    9. Fly style 'bout makin' choices that promote yo' whole self.

    10. Fly style attract what you need and what you want.

Ms. Fly don't need a man to take care of her. Successful men find that attractive. I guess some men get tired of bein' nothin' but a way to make a livin'.

Ms. Thang's Guide to Fly

Ms. Hoochie Self-image

1. Hoochie style either play up or ignore yo' physical features.

2. Hoochie style say you a one-dimensional person.

3. Hoochie style say you don't think enough of yo'self to earn someone else's respect.

Promotin' Yo'self

4. Hoochie style keep you on the low rung of the corporate ladder, if you on that ladder at all.

5. Hoochie style stop people from helpin' you achieve, 'cause they think you goin' to sleep yo' way to the top, anyway.

6. Hoochie style take the focus off of yo' capability and put it on yo' appearance.

Relationships

7. Hoochie style tell him that it might not be free, but it probably ain't worth much.

8. Hoochie style say you want to make sure ev'rybody know what you got to offer up front and hangin' out all over the place—seein' as you ain't nothin' but 1D (one-dimensional) anyway.

9. Hoochie style say, "look at me," not, "get to know me."

10. Hoochie style attract bustas and scare off the good men—the Spencers.

Bringin' It Home

Now, don't get me wrong—Hoochie style can and do attract reg'lar paycheck money, if you into old geezers lookin' for skeezers. This here a services-rendered relationship. Ain't nothin' in this type of relationship for you, 'ceptin' the money. 'Nother thang 'bout hoochie style is that it send out signals that you can be used. Ms. Thang's last word, hoochie style say "BLUE-LIGHT SPECIAL," no matter how much it cost.

Look here, Ms. Thang ain't here to give no fashion tips. Like I say, fly ain't all 'bout what you look like on the ouside. We 'bout to get into the principles of original fly in a minute.

First off, we got to start at the beginnin'.

Mainly, we been talkin' 'bout what fly is not, so ya'll ought to know by now. Befo' we get to specifics of what fly is, I got to tell you what I learned from my grandson—I'm talkin' 'bout my Netta's youngest boy.

Ms. Thang's Guide to Fly

Ain't nobody in this country ain't heard of Walt Disney. Netta's boy been workin' at the theme park in Florida. He call me up after he went through his trainin', got to tell grandma 'bout how his story great. Ain't tryin' to brag, Ms. Thang jest tellin' like it happen. Anyway, one thang my grandson said that stuck in my mind is that Mickey's daddy had this sayin' they all had to learn: Dream, Believe, Dare, Do. At the mouse house, they all got to know this, 'cause they say it's what makes them successful.

Well, I can get with that. Ms. Thang got her own sayin' come out of the original principles of fly. You want to be fly? Girl, you got to Dream, Believe, Reach, Achieve, Become and Teach.

Ain't no disrespect to Mr. Walt. He got his way. I got mine.

Walt had it right with the dreamin' part. We all got dreams, some folk jest ain't got no belief that they dreams can come true.

Some of us need to work on the believin' befo' we can dream.

Believe in what?

I'm not talkin' 'bout the spiritual now. I got my beliefs, I'm sure you got yours. Ms. Thang talkin' 'bout believin' in yo'self enough to know that you can reach the dreams you dare to dream.

I can't tell you what to dream, all I can do is give you a map for dreamin'.

You wanna' be fly? Believe in yo' dreams.

Aine A. Thang

Awright, I'm 'bout to break you off some thousand-dollar knowledge. Folks pay good money for speakers to tell them what you 'bout to get here, baby. Listen up. Girl, you ain't gettin' nowhere if you don't know where you want to go.

I know it sound easy, but it's the actin' that's hard.

I see it all the time. Girls got it goin' on every kind of way but believin'. They waitin' and waitin' for somebody to come and help them be, all the time, never realizin' that they already are.

You know what I'm sayin'?

I'm here, usin' up my old age to speak to a generation of folks ain't got no idea what fly 'bout. I figure they a lot of folks out there needin' to hear what I got to say. I figure they a lot of folks out there full of special fire, fly fire and they waitin' for sombody to come along and fan they fire.

Well, Ms. Girl, I'm here with the spark.

You need to burn up, baby girl. Glow. Flame. Rage out of control with yo' talent.

Maybe you the one to carry the knowledge of fly into the next generation.

Maybe.

Take more than one body to reach the ones comin' after. Ms. Thang lookin' for some diva-help, now.

Look, I'm tryin' to lead you somewhere good, girl. I'm tryin' to help you get yours so you can help somebody else get theirs.

It's like this—Harriet Tubman was the original Moses. She led folk to freedom. Ms. Thang is the new Moses. Granny

Ms. Thang's Guide to Fly

Fly, they call me 'round my place. Granny Fly ain't leadin' slaves to freedom.

You already free.

Maybe you don't know that.

Maybe 'I'm free' something you got to repeat three or four times while bangin' yo' heels together.

I don't know; but, one thang Granny Fly do know is this, ain't nobody in this world can hold you back, 'cept yo'self.

You as free as you gonna' get, girl.

Know that.

Once you know it, live it.

Ms. Thang ain't leadin' the freedom train. I'm leadin' the success train. Get on board with that spark you got inside. There's room for plenty 'board the success train. An' if you gettin' on Ms. Thang train, you keep in mind that room-for-plenty business.

Ain't nothin' rile Granny Fly mo' than folks thinkin' you got to get yo' success at the expense of other folk.

That jest ain't so.

There's room for you, room for me, and plenty room for anybody else want to hitch they star on the success train. Jest know this one thing: To get a ticket on Ms. Thang train, you got to commit yo'self:

Commit yo'self to dream;

Commit yo'self to believe;

Commit yo'self to reach;

Commit yo'self to achieve;

Commit yo'self to become; and, most important of all;

Commit yo'self to the return—come back fo' others once you made yo' success.

It's all good then.

Course, that's a lot of committin'.

But the committin' come one thang at a time. When you ready.

Right now, the only thang you got to commit to is takin' some time to dream. Like I said before, a lot of folks don't get what they want from life 'cause they ain't willin' to admit to theyselves jest what it is that they do want.

They don't know how to dream.

If you don't know how to dream, then you might as well take whatever life give you. After all, you ain't got no expectations nohow.

Course, fly don't think like that.

Girl, you can't make yo' world better if you ain't got no vision of better. *Better* start with a dream.

So what if the dream bigger than you can believe. Girl, the rule of dreamin' fly go like this: Dream big, plan small.

Ain't nobody like to climb a mountain all at one time. It jest ain't possible. Some dreams take baby steps; some dreams come together at the same time, but all dreams start with you taking the time to think 'bout what you truly want in this life.

Now, I know some things take time to change; some things can't ever be changed, but the truly fly know that you live, or die, based on the pieces of your soul that nurture or that you give away. That's why fly is all 'bout takin' who you are—the good inside you—and multiplyin' it. Nobody got control over

Ms. Thang's Guide to Fly

yo' inside 'ceptin' you.

Nobody can bring out the value you have as Ms. Fly 'ceptin' you.

Folk can help you develop.

Folk can help you get better at what you do.

But nobody can help you dream.

C'mon, Ms. Girl, hear me right.

Our best dreams come from the inside. Those are the dreams that God give us power enough to reach. Lot of folks tryin' to reach somebody else's dream for they life.

You do that, you givin' away yo' soul power.

If you studied yo' history, ya'll ought to know that slavery ain't bein' crushed and beaten by a master's whip.

True slavery is havin' yo' dreams shackled.

True fly is havin' the courage to dream, no matter what yo' physical situation.

There's power in dreamin'.

Generations of us benefittin' now from what other folks dreamed up in they minds: cars, phones, movie shows, and physical freedom for all, no matter what they color.

What dream you got hidin' inside of you?

Got to dream it to know it.

Think about yo' life. Think 'bout how things are in yo' life. Do you got it like you want it? If not, what do you really want?

Do you know?

Now, like I said befo', I can't help you dream. I don't aim to try. But, if you ain't never let yo'self dream befo', maybe I can help point you in the right direction.

First off, though, deal with the mind.

You deal with the mind 'cause yo' mind ain't necessarily lookin' out for you. Most of the time, folks operate on habit. Habit come from the way you was raised; and it come from where you learned what you know.

Ya'll know how it go. You want to do somethin' that you know is good for you, but, because of habit, yo' mind tellin' you that this good thang is stupid. Maybe yo' mind is tellin' you that this good thang ain't for you. After all, it's a good thang. Good thangs for other folks: for blonde-haired, blue-eyed folks, or dark-skinned chicks, or, everybody but you.

Yo' own mind is makin' you feel like you don't deserve what you dreamin' on. Girl, thinkin' like that put you on the wrong side of crazy. Thinkin' like that done caused a lot of folk to either not try for they dreams, or to mess up what they do try for.

Hear me? Girl, habit is hard to break; that's why fly deal with the mind first.

Flip the script on wrong-crazy, on the *can't, don't, won't*.

Watch Oprah; get some *believe-in-yo'-dream* audio tapes, whatever, but don't ignore yo' own negativism; otherwise, that negative thinkin' will raise up on the back side and try to destroy yo' dreams.

If you don't do Oprah, cause she jest ain't real enough for you, then at least fight back. When yo' mind tellin' you you can't, put yo' dukes up. Talk crazy right. Tell yo'self why you can. Make tellin' off yo' negative self into a habit.

Ms. Thang's Guide to Fly

Tell yo'self why you can achieve what you want to achieve. Don't put up with somethin' from yo'self that you wouldn't put up with from somebody else.

Awright? Ya'll know Granny Fly preachin' good word.

Now, the next thang you got to do to deal with the mind, is to give yo'self the right to dream.

I'm makin' it official, Ms. Fly-In-Training, you are now an authorized dreamer.

Do yo' dreamin' right, now. The only way to dream fly, is to write yo' dreams down.

Ain't no pressure to reach yo' dreams, not right now. Ain't no call to tell nobody yo' dreams. And, ain't no reason that you got to justify yo' dreams.

You jest makin' wishes in writin'.

Start off with the easy stuff: What's yo' dream for where you want to live?

What're yo' phyical needs: food, clothing, that kind of thing (Do you like designer labels on yo' threads, or do you style ghetto-fabu)?

Think 'bout what kind of people you want 'round you (fly of course). What do you want these people to think about you?

What do you want to do with yo' life?

This here dreamin' based on some kind of theory of somethin'. I don't know; I fell asleep durin' that part of the television show. All I know is that this fella' name of Abram Maslow put together a list of what folk need to be satisfied in life. Maslow's list been called the hierarcy of needs.

Don't know why they call it a theory, though. Us grandmas

been knowin' 'bout the hierarchy of need since before time start. We got our own name for it, call it: hon.

That's why you always hear grandmas sayin', "Tell Grandma, hon. What you need?"

And ya'll thought *hon* was short for honey.

Now you know.

And now you know 'bout writin' them dreams down on paper, too.

Ain't hard.

You got the goods. The fact that you read this far in my book mean you got somethin' inside you—that spark of original fly that make you special.

You weren't scared off when I was talkin' 'bout discipline and hard work.

You got desire.

It's bible, girl: 20 percent of folks doin' with they lives and the rest, 80 percent, jest strivin' and survivin'. Ms. Thang got a flash for you: survivin' ain't livin'. It's waitin' to die.

Too many folks dyin' in this world ain't never had a chance to live. Jest waitin' to die is a sorry way to live.

Mick ears, now.

You here for a purpose.

You got somethin' to do in this world and, that somethin' to do is more than jest gettin' up in the mornin' and makin' it through to another day.

You supposed to live yo' life, Ms. Fly.

Live it well.

By the way, you want to get started on making good roads

Ms. Thang's Guide to Fly

in yo' life, then, if you ain't done it yet, take a hot, little minute to write down yo' dreams.

Writin' yo' dreams down is important. I'll show you later how to get from dreamin' to settin' goals and, then, livin' yo' dreams. But first, you got to ink them dreams. If you ain't willin' to take the time to write 'em down, how you gonna' keep a check on yo'self?

Writin' it down keep you honest.

Writin' it down help you be disciplined.

Bein' discplined is a good thang but, then, what Ms. Thang got to say 'bout discipline a whole 'nother chapter.

CANE SENSE

- God created sex to be a good thang.

- You got to believe in yo'self to be able to dream.

- Write down yo' dreams. Then you on the way to livin' fly, baby girl.

Ms. Thang Speaks

The Disciplines of Fly

CHAPTER 4
▼
The Disciplines of Fly

> Girl, I don't wanna' hear no complaints 'bout fleas if you out there wavin' yo'self 'round like a t-bone steak and shoutin' "here boy," when a mongrel come barkin' 'round yo' door.

These the kind of days where folk jest tryin' to slide by quick as they can. Do anythin' to make a buck—even if it means sellin' they self-respect.

That's how they trainin' they kids, too. You see little kids apin' grown folk, tryin' to look hard, tryin' to look hot, tryin' to look cheap fly, little ones that don't know nothin' 'bout nothin'; but, since sex sells to hound dogs an' fools, why not get ev'rybody in on the act?

Sellin' yo' self-respect might make you rich, but after you done got yo' money, then what? You can't buy self-respect.

Come on, now, Ms. Thang speakin' truth. I ain't tryin' to dog nobody out. I ain't tryin' to preach no sermon, I'm jest droppin' some good knowledge. I'm givin' you the money worth right here. Ms. Thang tellin' the way thangs is.

Black Grandma Talkin', so listen up. To get to original fly, you need to hold on to yo' self-respect. Stay a hoochie and you steady explainin' the mistakes of yo' youth.

That's a hard fact. Most people don't want to be tryin' to act all sexy when they eighty-six. It's bad enough when these young banters go 'round lookin' hoochie but, Glory to God, some women ain't seem to know when to grow up, they thirty, forty, fifty, and still tryin' to look like springtime hoochie.

Do what you want. G-up to whatever you think you s'posed to be; but, Ms. Thang here to tell you that sex appeal ain't got nothin' to do with wearin' low-cut outfits that show off yo' buttercups—no matter how cute you think they are. If I shouldn't ought to do it at eighty-six, don't that mean I shouldn't ought to do it at twenty-five, thirty, or any age?

I don't see no reason why the young ought to be able to do somethin' jest 'cause they young. It ain't like they know more than a grown woman. They sho' ain't got mo' experience with life.

If it ain't a good look for you at eighty-six, then, girl, think hard befo' you doin' it at thirty-six.

Earlier, I was talkin' 'bout discipline. I ain't nowhere near talked enough 'bout discipline.

A body can't talk 'bout fly without talkin' 'bout discipline. Discipline one of the main foundations of fly.

Now when I say discipline, I ain't talkin' 'bout slappin' nobody upside they fool head. All discipline mean is doin' what you need to do, when you need to do it.

Simple enough.

Master discipline and you master yo' life.

Ain't nothin' I got to say mo' important than that one

thing right there.

All right?

All right.

Now, hold up. I got to speak to my peoples for a minute.

Discipline, my people... discipline.

That's a money word.

How you think black folks been thrivin', not jest survivin'?

From Reconstruction to lynchin', we s'posed to been done failed, but my people had the discipline to get up and keep on steppin' ev'rytime life tried to knock us down.

Survivin' ain't nothin' but a thang. Thrivin', now that require discipline.

An' I tell you somethin' else: discipline a gift you give to yo'self. You master discipline, then add a little dream to it, girl, that's all you need. 'Cept maybe some of my buttermilk cornbread and a tall glass of iced tea. You got all that, you good to go. The cornbread give you energy. Wash it down with the tea an' call me in the mornin'.

I'm jest kiddin' 'bout the food, but Ms. Thang don't play when I'm talkin' 'bout dreams.

Hear me? Get discipline and, girl, you bakin' up success right there.

I got to be real, now.

There might be detours; true. There might be changes; true. There might be failures and there might be issues; true, and true. But long as you headin' in the direction you want to go, it don't matter if you take the scenic route. Discipline will get you there and get you there with yo' self-respect.

Don't get me wrong, now, Ms. Thang ain't so backward that I don't know nothin' but what's in front of my face.

I know ain't nothin' a man like better'n than a Hoochie—leastwise, some men; the smart ones leave well enough alone. A few of the good ones get caught up and burned ev'ry now and again; but, most men sniffin' 'round hoochies ain't much better than hounds.

Girl, I don't wanna' hear no complaints 'bout fleas if you out there wavin' yo'self 'round like a t-bone steak and shoutin' "here boy," when a mongrel come barkin' 'round yo' door.

Ain't no excuse for it, girl. A hound will jump whatever is squattin'; it don't make no difference to him.

All that information they got out there 'bout crazy diseases, girl, you oughta' know you got to be careful these days. You hangin' where you ought to hang, you won't need that heavy-duty flea collar.

All right? You hearin' me, Ms. Too-Much-Stuff?

I hope so. I hope you learnin' somethin' to help you make yo' way, maybe even help you snag yo'self a worthy fella', if that's what you want.

After all, if you aimin' to be original fly, you ain't got time for scratchin' fleas.

Speakin' 'bout the hounds on prowl, girl, you know that there more single women in this country than single men—least in the generation roamin' the streets right now.

That there ought to let you know that if you lookin' for a man, any man, you got to have some skills.

Ms. Thang's Guide to Fly

If you lookin' for a good man, you got to be fly like original fly.

A lot of women single 'cause they ain't got not even one good piece of sense up in they bubble heads.

Some women might as well be single, but they with the wrong man, for all the wrong reasons.

For you hoochies ain't 'bout to change for nobody, not even yo'self, Ms. Thang got a word for you, too. Girl, even if you ain't lookin' for no promises from a man, you still gotta have some skills on yo' resume.

Ain't no way you can compete on them falsies alone.

But that kind of relationship ain't what Ms. Thang talkin' 'bout.

We talkin' 'bout original fly. Between you and me, you want to profile fly, then you got to bust up them excuses.

Ms. Fly ain't got time for makin' no excuses.

Ms. Fly ain't waitin' for nobody come glidin' by with a silver tray so she can pick her heart desire off of it. For all she know, the waiter might skip her table.

Mick ears, girl, I'm tellin' you like I told my own girls. If you want to be fly, then don't be lookin' for a man to do for you. You do for yo'self.

And, Ms. Thang got some more fly knowledge for you all. I been talkin' 'bout bein' disciplined. Well, that's all right and true, but you got to know what all that means.

Aine A. Thang

Ms. Thang's Disciplines of Fly

1. Discipline is doin' what need to be done, when it need to be done.

2. Discipline is 'bout keepin' yo' promises to yo'self. You say you 'bout somethin', then be 'bout it.

3. Discipline is 'bout gettin' up and startin' over if somethin' don't go right. Ain't never heard nobody say Ms. Fly got to be perfect. All I heard was practice make perfect.

4. Discipline is 'bout keepin' on the path you set for yo'self. Keep hold of principles and values less'n you learn somethin' new that make yo' old values flat-out wrong.

Put them big Mickey ears on and hear me right: Master discipline. Ain't hard to master the meaning of discipline. One mo' time, 'til you sick of hearin' it, do what you need to do, when you need to do it. That's good knowledge. Discipline make a whole world of difference betwixt hoochie and fly.

Ms. Thang's Guide to Fly

CANE SENSE:

- Master discipline and you master yo' life.
- If you lookin' for a man, any man, girl, you got to have some kind of skills.
- Ms. Fly ain't got no time for makin' excuses.
- Girl, know the disciplines of true fly.

Ms. Thang Speaks

Attractin' Spencers

CHAPTER 5
▼

Attractin' Spencers

Girl, the first step in attractin' the right kind of man is knowin' the difference between the right kind and the wrong.

Eleven Quick Ways to Spot a Busta

1. He talk, but don't listen. You the lovely lady drivin' Busta crazy. Uh huh. Give him what he need, girl, but is Busta listenin' to what you need? Hope so. That's his job if he's yo' man.

2. He want a quarterly financial report an' income statement. Remember what I said 'bout a man bein' a way to make a livin'? Well that cut both ways. If he a busta, then you his day job. If the man ain't got no kind of job, then cut him loose. And don't spend no time listenin' to him jaw on how he can't get no kind of break.

3. Busta dropped out of school and never dropped back

in. Learnin' is the key. But, then again, maybe you got a busta with a degree. Before you start in on how smart B of A Busta is, peep this: Knowledge is what you learn, but wisdom is usin' what you know. He gotta be wise to hold on to a fly girl like you.

4. Busta doin' drugs. One mo once, girl. Ain't nobody got to tell you that ain't a ride you want to be on. Bust that busta, quick time and walk.

5. One mo once, girl. You oughta' know he ain't right if his best friend a bottle of brew.

6. Ditto, if destruction is his game, and he think the only true power is gun power. Ditch and run.

7. Busta can't conversate 'bout nothin' 'cept how much he want you. Girl, he might want you, but after he got you, then what? Ms. Fly need a man with some dreams beyond the sheets. Bein' with a man ain't got no dreams is like bein' in a desert at night without water. The heat cools, but you still gonna' die of thirst.

8. Ditto, busta always conversatin' 'bout how "the man" is always gettin' over on us. Hmph! The man got over on ev'rybody, but I only know a few people still holdin' theyselves down 'cause of it. Learn the history of yo'

Ms. Thang's Guide to Fly

people, fly girl. If you don't like that history, then do what you can to make sure it don't never happen again. If you find somethin' good, then fan that flame in yo' own heart. Pick up that left-behind legacy and run with it. I came up when White folks still thought we ought to be under 'em, but we overcame, and we overcomin' now. Don't you let what other people believe stop you from gettin' yo' props. You make a way for yo'self in spite of. It's what our people did when I was young. We had doctors and lawyers and policemen, and it was surely harder back then than it is now. Now you got some Black folks sayin' that the reason we can't is 'cause Black role models ain't livin' in the 'hood. An excuse ain't nothin' but an excuse. Bustas make excuses. Fly don't. Don't be a busta. You want to hang? Then—Focus. Hang. Win. 'Cause that's the way it go.

9. Busta ain't willin' to stand up for you with his family. If the boy ain't got the guts to tell his Momma to treat you with respect, then chuck the chump. Now, I ain't sayin' that you can treat his momma any kind of way. Give her the dap. Respect is a two-way street, but if his Momma is smart, she won't go dippin' in yo' business. If her baby is big enough to be mackin, then he big enough to face up to his Momma. 'Sides, that boy gonna' have bigger battles than his Momma to face. She jest the first hurdle to him becomin' a real

man. Ya'll know that if a mother love her son the way she should, she'll accept you—less'n you a hoochie.

10. Busta got bills all over the place and don't know nothin' 'bout a one of 'em. On top of that, he always borrowin' money from you to pay his way.

11. The number one sign of a Busta: Got kids all over the place and don't know nothin' 'bout a one of 'em.

Girl, the first step in attractin' the right kind of man is knowin' the difference between the right kind and the wrong.

Bringin' It Home:

It's time for my girls to rise up and demand the respect they deserve. Hey-ay! Ain't not one thing wrong with brown skin—no matter how light or dark. We didn't get too much from the seventies, but we did learn that bein' Black is a beautiful thing. Since I'm gettin' closer to Glory ev'ry day, I have to chase them rabbits as I can, so let me take a minute to talk 'bout bein' part of the Black race.
 Yes, we came over here from Africa—probably befo' Columbus. I'm proud of my roots, but bein' Black ain't 'bout nothin' but puttin' a category on folks—puttin' a box 'round 'em.
 Listen up. Wearin' kente clothe and headwraps don't

Ms. Thang's Guide to Fly

make you one iota Blacker than you were befo' you got dressed.

All that stuff jest showin' respect for the African culture. I'd be the last to talk against it, 'cause showin' appreciation for yo' culture a good thang, but ain't nothin' holy 'bout havin' a Blacker-than-thou thing. 'Specially not when you use that to put yo'self above yo' sister or brother—no matter how Eurocentric you may think they are.

Ain't nothin' make a body more irritable than to hear one of they own people tellin' another one that they ain't Black enough. If you don't like prejudice, then don't be prejudiced. When God painted my canvas, he didn't say nothin' 'bout my havin' to be a card-carryin' member of the "Blacker-than-thou club." If He don't work that way, then why should you?

Can I get a witness to my pain?

So, it don't matter how sidditty, how proud, how nothin' yo' Black brother or sister is. They may be livin' in the suburbs all wrapped in luxury, but you ain't walked in they shoes. You don't know where they at until you willin' to give them the space to have they say. 'Course, that cut both ways. You give respect and get it back, 'specially to yo' own. Don't matter if they married to someone so White you think it's snowin'! Ain't none of us gettin' nowhere without each other, and that means you judge a man by the color of his heart.

Judge a man or woman that way, then they may help you move yo' own dreams forward.

All right, you got the breakdown on bustas, so here's the Ms. Thang's information hotline on the right kind of man.

Aine A. Thang

Ten Ways to Spot a Spencer

1. He want to know 'bout you and what's goin' on in yo' mind.

    Spencer make the effort to see you as more than his sweet thang. To Spencer, you a person with thoughts and feelin's. He take the time to think on yo' needs, not jest his own. For him to do that, the boy got to ask questions and listen to the answers. Ain't nobody perfect, but this here an important part of buildin' marriages that last. If he ain't 'bout to listen, then he ain't 'bout to meet the needs you got inside you. Matter fact, he ain't 'bout nothin' but hisself.

2. Spencer keep his eye on the money flow.

    Some folk want to believe that a man that know how much he got in his bank account too tight with a dollar bill, but the truth of the matter is that Spencer keepin' his eye open on what he got, and he keepin' up with where what he got go. Sho' you can over-do countin' pennies like they was worth somethin', but a true Spencer know he got to manage his stuff. Managin' the only way to keep what he got and make it grow. Brother got his subscription to *Black Enterprise* and readin' it from page to page. Take yo' eye off yo' money, and that money will take off.

3. Jest like busta can't take the time to put something in his mind beyond dopin and ropin', Spencer got it goin' on in the I.Q. department.

I ain't sayin' Spencer got to be Einstein, but Spencer ain't got his brain confused with his manhood. Too many Black men get labeled Poindexters when they ain't doin' nothin' but tryin' to put somethin' inside theyselves to help them get on. Education gettin' folk out of the ghetto and into the 'burbs. Call him Poindexter if you want, but Spencer usin' that muscle up in his head, makin' it grow so that he can apply it to bein' a good influence. 'Course, if the only thing the man bendin' in his mind is how to get over on somebody, then you ought to know he a busta.

4. Spencer take care of hisself for his baby.

Awright, now, Spencer puttin' some effort into lookin' good for his woman. I ain't sayin' he wearin' a tuxedo to dinner, all I'm sayin' is that Spencer thinkin' 'bout the future and it show in the way he take care of his physical self. Goes without sayin', if you read up on how to spot a busta, you know Spencer keepin' his temple free from drugs, alcohol abuse, and sexual diseases.

5. You the woman he thinkin' 'bout when he put on his Aqua V.

Goin' along with takin' care of hisself, Spencer elephant-faithful, girl, one-hundred percent. Reason Spencer a good man, 'cause he ain't spreadin' hisself 'cross the planet like artery-cloggin' margarine. Mr. S. a one-woman man, not a one-at-a-time man.

6. Spencer handle his responsibilities.

He don't need somebody workin' on him 'bout what he should and shouldn't do. Spencer a grown man, and a grown man take his responsibilities serious. When you plannin' with yo' man, you ain't got to keep checkin' up on him like he some little boy, 'cause he show you with his actions that you can trust him. Discipline is doin' what need to be done, when it need to be done. Spencer got discipline enough, he tell hisself what to do. And, he understand that he in a relationship that require him to make some effort. Ain't nothin' worse than listenin' to a man complain 'bout doin' what he s'posed to do. With Spencer, you don't even have to ask, baby girl. First he said it, then he did it.

Ms. Thang's Guide to Fly

7. Spencer proud of his woman.

   He proud to have you on his arm. Spencer take his woman anywhere. He ain't always tryin' to make you stay at home while he out paintin' the town with his friends. Girl, you ain't got to wonder where Spencer at 'cause he ain't tryin' to prove nothin' to nobody but you.

8. Spencer got a hold on his temper.

   In this day an' age, ain't nobody should have to worry 'bout gettin' beat up by the man who s'posed to be they soul-mate. The man that lay a hand on you a busta. Spencer treat his woman with love and respect.

9. Spencer ain't too proud to work a job beneath his skill.

   I know it's a new millennium. (Seems like I been here for most of the last century—and I gotta mind to stay a little bit longer. Mayhap I'll be writin' my memoirs when I reach one hundred. We'll see.) I know the world changin', but some of it changin' fast, some of it changin' slow. From what I know, seem a lot of folk workin' beneath what they can do. That's how it happen sometimes. You pay yo' dues. But while Spencer doin' what he got to do to take care of business, he also makin' plans. Ain't no excuse for not havin' no plan for yo' life, 'cept ignorance. Spencer know bein' Black ain't no excuse. Bein' poor ain't no excuse. Bein' a woman ain't no excuse. Heck, bein' a hoochie ain't no excuse neither. If you aimin' to be fass an' nasty, you might as well make a plan to be fass and nasty and livin' large, too. A lot of folks doin' jest that, they got theyselves they own city, call it Hollywood. Awright, it's time for me to leave them folks alone and get back on to fly. Look. Poor folks, Black folks, women folks, Fly Chicks and, yes, even hoochies, reachin' they dreams. Sometime the dream come to 'em easy, sometime it come hard, but the only way to make sure it come is to have that dream mapped out.

10. Spencer got hisself a plan for his life.

In fact, havin' a plan so important, I think I'll make it number ten on the list of what you want that man to be 'bout. Girl, ain't nothin' so fly like havin' a man who goin' somewhere. A man got a vision you can join up and work together on, that's powerful stuff, there. Some of the strongest marriages a result of shared vision. Ain't always happen but, when it do, watch out. You got somethin' that can change yo' world.

Ms. Thang's Guide to Fly

CANE SENSE

- Girl, you need to know how to spot a busta. Check out my list on the signs to know when it's time to hit gas and get gone.

- Be proud of yo' roots, girl, but understand that race ain't nothin' but a box to put 'round folks. Don't go tryin' to use race like some kind of excuse to keep you from gettin' to yo' dream. That's jest flat out wrong.

- Jest like you need to know a busta when you see him, girl, you need to know when Mr. Right knockin' on yo' door. From Busta to Spencer, now you got the A-to-Z knowledge on men.

Ms. Thang Speaks

As Fly As You Wanna' Be

CHAPTER 6
▼

As Fly As You Wanna' Be

If folk can look at you and know whether you an 'innie" or an "outie," and whether you like Playtex or Victoria Secret, you a little on the ripe side of desperate.

This here a generation of folk always wantin' a survey to prove what they already know. Can't nobody do nothin' these days without askin' what other folk think.

Well, Ms. Thang got yo' survey. I know ya'll think old folk don't know nothin', but we invented knowin', so ya'll can jest give Ms. Thang some respect on faith.

Anyway, I heard tell this one survey askin' men what they liked 'bout women they wanted to marry. We ain't talkin' 'bout gettin' wit' it. This here the bona fide, good-to-go, got-the-ring-on-yo'-ring-finger kind of love. What surprise me is that ain't nown one of them men say they like hoochies.

What they did like had to do with a woman bein' fly like I been droppin' knowledge 'bout. It had to do with her attitude, behavior, and how she presentin' herself.

Real men and real women ain't like what they showin' on TV, but too many folk buyin' what they see and tryin' to live they lives like Temptation Island a real place.

Aine A. Thang

When I was comin' up, we listened to the radio. They told all kinds of stories, almost make you believe the stories were really happenin', but no matter how real that stuff seem, we didn't get confused 'bout what was real and what was fake.

Couldn't nobody afford to forget the difference. Back in the day, forgettin' real was liable to get a body in all kinds of trouble.

Let Granny Fly break it down nice and easy: Real is what you doin' day to day.

Real ain't make nothin' happen for you 'less you doin' to make somethin' happen.

What dream you workin' for?

That's what I want to know.

Talkin' 'bout this generation, ya'll got so many books that can teach you what you need to know 'bout gettin' what you want, seem like you ought not need Ms. Thang speakin' out on the subject. And maybe you don't want to hear what I got to say, but I still got to testify to what I'm seein'.

Ev'ry weekend my granddaughter come and get me and we go walkin', "a little jaunt in the park," my granddaughter call it, like she think we in England. That's awright, though. Least she comin' to visit. I ain't got no complaints.

Anyhow, I see so many young girls, girls as beautiful as they want to be, and they all stuffed into clothes so tight, you'd think they was sausages tryin' to fit into the casin'.

Don't get me wrong, I ain't sayin' nobody ought to go 'round lookin' five-and-dime. Ms. Thang a church woman—still make it to the church when I can. Ya'll know us church women

Ms. Thang's Guide to Fly

like to get dipped on a Sunday.

Yes, we do.

An' I miss those days when we got to step out, hats on, dressed in our Sunday best to the Glory of God, but them days ain't like nowadays. These days, folks ain't so formal. Maybe that's a good thing, it ain't my right to say.

What I do know is that there's a difference betwixt fashion and fass.

Some of these girls I be seein' in the park got too much fass an' not enough fashion; the upshot of it bein', instead of lookin' fly, they lookin' desperate.

Come correct now, ya'll ought to know that dressin' hoochie ain't nothin' but lookin' desperate. I mean, girls walkin' 'round lookin like they got a sign on they forehead jest screamin' 'can't kill nothin', won't nothin' die.'

Lookin' desperate akin to sendin' out a fresh meat scent, an' ain't nothin' but hounds sniffin' the air. A hound can smell desperate a mile away.

I know somebody out there right now flappin' they lips, talkin' 'bout how Ms. Thang don't know.

That may be.

Let me break you off some grown woman knowledge, and we'll see.

Aine A. Thang

Five Signs That You Profilin' Desperation:

1. Girl, you givin' God and ev'rybody free pookie peeks. If folk can look at you and know whether you an 'innie" or an "outie," and whether you like Hanes Her Way bra or Victoria Secret, you a little on the ripe side of desperate.

2. Girl, you past ripe if yo' Momma' worried you gonna' get brain-damage from that hard jiggle in yo' step.

3. Girl, you hittin' rotten if folk think you work for the fire department cause you all over town steady puttin' out men's fires.

5. Girl, you know you desperate if you think goin' out in public mean you s'posed to get undressed and advertise jest why yo' number on the bathroom wall.

6. Girl, you know you desperate if you spend all yo' time hard-lippin' folks for tryin' to squeeze into outfits you got in yo' closet right now. Don't matter the shape. If you can wear it, so can they. If they ain't ought to wear it, why should you? 'Cause skinny better? Say who? Fly ain't 'bout size, now. Don't get fooled.

Ms. Thang's Guide to Fly

Granny Fly hard linin', now. I'm tryin' to show you a better way. Ms. Thang might be gone tomorrow. I got to teach what I can while I can.

Listen and learn, baby girl. Girl, if the only bank you got is yo' body, you 'bout broke. True fly a reflection of what you got built up on the inside—not what you look like. That inside fly will show itself on the outside, too. Have somethin' good inside you to show the world.

Like I said befo', Temptation Island a TV show. Don't be playin' reruns like you ain't gonna' get hurt. You in the real world. Ain't no camera 'round here to show yo' heartbreak and help you get a million dollar contract on daytime TV.

Hear me right, Golden Child, Ms. Thang ain't got nothin' against style and fashion. Fashion ain't my line of work. Even so, I know the difference between fashionable and fass.

I ain't givin' tips now, cause I don't claim to be no fashion maven. You want style tips, pick up *Essence* magazine, but know this: Black women been creatin' style since back in the day.

From my way of thinkin', if you a Black woman, you belong to a race of people got a legacy of style. Don't trash yo' heritage by lookin' trashy.

You settin' style for generations to come. Do it right.

Now that you got my word on all that, I reckon I should get back to the original subject. Ms. Thang started off talkin' 'bout surveys. Accordin' to that one survey, this here what men thought of as attractive in they women:

Aine A. Thang

1. Confidence
2. Lookin' to see the good-side of thangs
3. Smilin' a lot
4. Puttin' they family up as important
5. Class
6. Bein' lovin'

Ain't none of them men say fass and nasty. They didn't even say sexy. Ain't nothin' on that list 'bout wearin' lots of makeup. The closest the list come to talkin' 'bout the outside of a woman is number five. And for you hoochies, class 'bout as far from fass and nasty as a body could get. Girl, how you gonna' have class if you ain't wearin' nothin' to cover yo'self?

Ain't no such bird as a classy hoochie.

Ya'll ain't got to believe Ms. Thang. Do yo' own research. Test how you get treated dressed as a hoochie then, test how you get treated dressed as somebody got some class. I expect you'll be findin' this information on the money.

Men don't like they women lookin' hoochie. Think 'bout it. They ain't wantin' they woman to go 'round lookin' like she for rent when she ain't.

Even in that movie, *Pretty Woman*, they didn't keep Julia Roberts lookin' like a hoochie. She was Cinderella made over into high class befo' the man fall in love with her.

Some folks forget ev'rythang 'bout the movie exceptin' the fact that Julia got herself a rich man.

'Course, it was jest a movie.

In real life, if you a hoochie, then, girl, some actor might stop and help you get yo' face in the newspaper for a minute or two, but he ain't stayin' 'round to read yo' memoirs.

One other interestin' thing 'bout the list was that they check how much money the men takin' the survey got. The ones with the most money were the ones most interested in a woman bein' somethin' 'sides an' empty-head with big flashlights. Girl, I'm tellin' you real. Dress like a hoochie and you jest might be throwin' away yo' opportunity to attract what you want.

An' if you still holdin' on to dressin' hoochie, then I don't expect you lookin' too hard for a Spencer.

CANE SENSE

- Girl, when you profilin' desperation, only thing you attractin' is hounds and vultures.

- Girl, contrary to what them flashy magazines tellin' you, men don't want they women runnin' round advertisin' they wares.

- Girl, if you ain't got no brain, them flashlights you shinin' on the world ain't like to get you nowhere but used and abused.

Ms. Thang Speaks

Leave It Alone

CHAPTER 7
▼

Leave It Alone

Don't tell Ms. Thang she don't know
'bout what it's like out in the real world.

Now, as I was sayin' befo'— I know you was hopin' I'd forget, but it took me too long to get here; Ms. Thang ain't forgettin' nothin' on her witness stand—be a proud sister. Don't jest lift up yo' voice, lift up yo' head, girl, and lift it high.

Let me give you Ms. Thang's two sure-fire ways to prove you as fly as you wanna be when it come to love:

1. Expect yo' man to find his path in life. God didn't put that man on earth for no good reason. Spencer got a purpose. He got somethin' to do with his life. God gave him gifts inside that he need to bring out. Maybe you s'posed to help him find that thing, maybe he already found it befo' the two of you hooked up. The point is, you got to be strong enough to help him be, then brave enough to let him be.

2. The same go for you. Don't jest sit at home bein' somebody's woman. You the first lady, baby. You got to get yo' platform in life. So you got babies you want to get raised first, ain't no shame in that. Folks so busy turnin' up they noses at mothers who stay at home, then turnin' up that same snot-filled nose at mothers who work. You start havin' babies, you don't always get to choose what you want. You deal with what you got.

After you done with the dealin', you got to ask yo'self if you accomplished yo' purpose. Ain't no tragedy worse that lettin' color, lettin' gender, lettin' anything stop you from fulfillin' what you been called to be. Didn't say it would be easy, but that's the journey. That's what life all 'bout. 'Til you know that, then you ain't livin'.

See, you ain't nothin' without the journey. You owe it to yo'self, to yo' man, and to yo' legacy to become the woman you was always meant to be.

Bein' the woman you s'posed to be, now, baby, that's fly.

Please, please don't let nobody tell you that fly is 'bout bein' 36-24-28. It ain't 'bout knowin' the latest dance moves, drinkin' ev'rybody under the table, or bein' able to take nobody's man, neither.

And don't tell Ms. Thang she don't know 'bout what it's like out in the real world. I ain't always been livin' in a nursin' home, and Ms. Thang been 'round long enough to teach all of

Ms. Thang's Guide to Fly

y'all 'bout trouble. Been there, done that, and sold my OWN t-shirts. Still, the thing is, we all end up in the same place. You live long enough, you'll be like me: old, tired, filled with regrets and memories.

I done had plenty of time to think back on missed turns in my life. A man can make you miss a turn. A man can make you choose the wrong thing. But befo' you choose, remember, he ain't got to live out yo' life—you do. Spencer ain't 'bout to ask you to make a wrong choice for him. Busta, on the other hand, always expectin' you to do what he want.

Awright, now, Ms. Thang got another list for you.

Aine A. Thang

Ten Reasons Why Bein' a Hoochie Hurt You

1. Bein' a Hoochie hurt yo' children. Those babies of yourn are yo' mark on the world. The way you live yo' life affect them. You teach yo' children that they gifts, and when you old and gray like I am, you might have someone comin' to visit you at the nursin' home. Teach 'em to live the life of a Hoochie and you settin' 'em up. They know who to blame. You jest makin' it harder for them to break the chain. I seen granbabies—not mine, thank the good Lord above—havin' babies. That ain't right. It's awful hard to think a'bout what you want when you got responsibilities like kids. It's ain't fair to you. It ain't fair to yo' babies, if you resentin' them for bein' there. Course, once they come, you love 'em and do yo' best to raise 'em with good sense. Even if you ain't start right, you can finish right. Jest know that after you have children, yo' life ain't jest 'bout what you want no more. It's 'bout what's good for you AND them babies you got. Don't let nobody tell you that you CAN'T. Life is all 'bout what choices you make. That might be the only power you have in life, but you can make choices that make yo' life better or worse. Makin' good choices is FLY.

Ms. Thang's Guide to Fly

2. Bein' a Hoochie hurt yo' friendships. Ain't nothin' better than the friendship of a sister—someone you can trust, someone who got yo' back. Hoochies ain't got friendships like that. Don't nobody trust a hoochie. They too busy makin' moves on ev'ry man in town.

3. Bein' a Hoochie hurt yo' chance to find real love. Ain't no such thing as real love without commitment. If he think you easy, then he jest whilin' his time. He ain't plannin' on the long haul. Men got conquerin' inside they DNA, girl. Be the mountain he got to work for—jest don't be impossible.

4. Bein' a Hoochie hurt yo' health. I won't even talk 'bout the diseases Hoochies get, and the stress: worryin' 'bout gettin' pregnant, worryin' 'bout takin' care of yo' babies, worryin' 'bout money. What's healthy 'bout that? Makin' good choices mean you got to be disciplined. You got to be focused on what you want, for yo'self and for people whose lives connect with yourn. Live long and prosper, girl. That's a lot easier to do when you livin' right—no matter how scary it feels.

5. Bein' a Hoochie destroy yo' self-esteem. Folks used to think that Black women was different from other women, that we didn't care 'bout bein' pretty. We

didn't care 'bout our families. Sound like we didn't care 'bout nothin'. Ya'll know that's a lie from the pit. Black women got feelin' jest like ev'rybody else. Our women do not need to be livin' the Hoochie lifestyle—leave that to them Cosmo girls got trust funds big enough to cover they bad choices. Fly style is built on good self-esteem. Self-esteem mean you got self-respect. Self-respect show in ev'ry area of yo' life, includin' the way you present yo'self. Respect yo'self. Hoochies don't.

6. Bein' a Hoochie hurt possibilities. Soon, it ain't the men you goin' to be workin' to please. It's other women. Women graduatin' from college faster than men. They startin' mo' companies than men. If you a Hoochie ain't got no skills, then you a Hoochie out of luck and out of touch with how to make yo' way in this world.

7. Bein' a Hoochie hurt yo' capabilities. You profile 1-D, and people ain't got time to help you find yo' way. They believe yo' profile: 1-D profile sayin' you ain't got the goods. You one-dimensional, outside only. You got to profile success, or at least potential, if you want help and a chance to develop yo'self.

8. Bein' a Hoochie hurt yo' credibility. Girl, if folks think you all a'bout takin' the easy way, they ain't a'bout to

Ms. Thang's Guide to Fly

call on you when they need somebody they can trust. You got to prove yo'self to folks. Provin' yo'self mean that when opportunity come along for you to make a choice, you use yo' mind and yo' talents to solve problems, not yo' customer-loyalty-key at the Cockroach Motel.

9. Bein' a Hoochie hurt yo' soul. Maybe you don't believe in the hereafter. Don't. But bein' that hot and heavy lasts for a minute and true love—a real heart-to-heart connection that stirs you up from the inside to the out and lasts a lifetime, somebody please tell me how a Hoochie, puttin' out to anybody can feed her soul.

   'Course, if you ain't got it like that, if you feel you ain't got no choices, and you puttin' out to be able to put food on the table, then you not really livin'. My advice to you is to do whatever you need to do to join us on the planet. It's worth the hard work.

10. Finally, bein' a Hoochie hurt yo' people. When I say yo' people, I don't mean yo' mama and yo' daddy. I mean all us women folk need one more good role model. I mean all us who need one more hand to help a brother or sister up.

    Black folk been tearin' up stereotypes for as long

as other folks been creatin' 'em, but this is one generation that seem to want to throw away the freedoms other folks won for 'em. In all my years, I ain't never heard so many excuses 'bout why folk ain't doin' and movin' as I hear from this generation.

All our rights—the right to vote, the right to freedom, the right to free speech—need protectin'. They ain't guaranteed. An', girl, you ain't protectin' 'em by actin' crazy with yo' freedom. Protect yo' rights by honor and by commitment of peoples who defend 'em. Don't hurt yo' people. Don't destroy yo' promise. Believe in yo'self. Reach. Achieve. And Become. You can do it.

CANE SENSE

- Girl, don't let nothin' stop you from bein' who you called to be. Might be hard, but that's where the learnin' come in. You learnin' so you can teach somebody else on the path.

- Girl, bein' a hoochie ain't nothin' but hurtin' yo'self. You need to respect yo'self and, the ones that came befo' you, fightin' so that you could live yo' life free.

- Girl, you might not got it like that, but if you don't, you

Ms. Thang's Guide to Fly

need to do whatever it take to get on the planet and live your life with purpose.

Ms. Thang Speaks

Or, Get It Together

CHAPTER 8
▼

Or, Get It Together

Don't destroy yo' promise.

The Hoochie Makeover

Ready for a change?

I been tryin' my best to help you realize that ain't nothin' good 'bout bein' a Hoochie.

'Course, I wouldn't no-how be surprised to see a book on the top-ten list with a title like "How to Embrace Yo' Hoochie Self."

This country has gone that far from good sense. Aside from the Hoochie shows, the next most popular talk show I been seein' is them makeover shows. So, Ms. Thang got yo' makeover, and it ain't nothin' but a thang to transform from hoochie to fly.

We done conversed 'bout original principles of fly. But jest in case you need a reminder:

Fly is **Focused** on reachin' yo' goals and makin' good choices.

Fly is **Lovin'** yo'self enough to surround yo'self with good influences and good people.

Fly is **You** takin' care of yo'self.
Got it?

We done talked 'bout attitude and how havin' the right attitude is one of the foundations of fly. So, to help you set yo' mind right, Ms. Thang goin' where no diva done gone befo'. Call me Grandma Tony Robbins, 'cause I got yo' mindset medicine right here.

Ms. Thang's Fly Mantra #1

> I will believe in possibilities.
> I will reach for my dreams.
> I will achieve my goals.
> I will become with purpose.
> I will teach others and leave a legacy.

Ms. Fly don't hide behind drugs. She don't use sex as a drug. Her life got meanin'. Ms. Woman makin' this world a better place to live.

That's original fly, baby girl. Original fly based on self-respect. Ms. Fly will return respect to those who give it to her.

Ms. Thang's Guide to Fly

Remember, it's yo' dreams and goals that make you real. You got to live expecting to reach them dreams. The path may be hard. The road may be long. The journey may require ev'ry ounce of courage you got, but you can achieve.

You fearfully and wonderfully made, baby girl. That mean you deserve good things in yo' life. You have the right to work for the things you want. You deserve a committed relationship with a good man.

Ms. Fly a woman with the goods, so she can attract a man with the goods.

Maybe you still thinkin' that a hoochie life the way to fly. I got you, too. If you want help for takin' the other route, here go the mantra from "Embracin' Yo Hoochie Self."

The Hoochie Mantra

It's too hard. I can't get ahead. You don't know me. You ain't got no business dippin' in my business. I'm tired. It wouldn't help anyway. Got to find me a man to take care of my needs.

Dream Crazy

You got hopes? You got dreams? No matter how much of a somebody you are, folks don't judge you by the fact that you are, they judge you by what you do with who you are.

Girl, pay attention, now. That's some knowledge worth holdin' on to. Fly sisters use they talents. This little light of mine, I'm gonna' let it shine.

Don't be hidin' yo' talents.

Shine.

Ain't talkin' 'bout showin' off. Ain't talkin' 'bout showin' folks up. I'm talkin' 'bout releasin' the fire and spirit inside you. That's the light you got to shine.

And know, Ms. Bright, that the shine ain't to make you look good. Shining lift you up so that other people can find they way. That's why the Word tell you to shine, girl.

It's a good thing.

Hear me right. I ain't talkin' 'bout packagin' now, I'm talkin' 'bout the inside light.

What's inside yo' box?

Later on, we gonna' talk 'bout how you can pick up on yo' purpose in life, but first, take a minute to go back and look at yo' dreams.

Like I said, yo' dreams what make you you.

Go over them dreams one mo' time. Later, we will move on to settin' goals, but first, put yo' dreams into categories. Think on yo' dreams this-a-way:

Write what you want in love/relationships.

Write what you want money-wise.

Write what you want spirit-wise.

Write what you want body-wise, yo' physical self.

Write anything you can think of.

Dream big.

Dream crazy.

Write it down.

Ms. Thang's Guide to Fly

You on Fantasy Island now. Santa Claus is comin' to town and he want you to beam him yo' I-been-a-good-girl list.

Ain't no shame in havin' dreams.

Dream as big and crazy as Martin Luther King, Jr.

Only way to move ahead in life is to dream. Girl, these dreams are yo' dream map. Yo' dream map showin' you the level of life you want.

Now ya'll know you can have a map of a city, but all the map show you is what the city got to offer. If you want to partake of the pleasures of that city, you got to make the effort to get yo'self where you want to be.

Plane, train, automobile, walk a thousand miles through the driftin' snow, you got the responsibility to get there.

For some, the hard part is the dreamin'. If you been doin' what I say, then you got that first step of dreamin' and writin' yo' dreams done.

There are some folk can't get nothin' done for spendin' all they time dreamin'. They dreamin', but, they ain't goin' nowhere. These the folk that need to learn how to put priority on they dreams.

To move from believin' to the reachin' stage, you got to join what you really want to do with yo' time, together with thought-out action.

Let me break it down like this, some of what you want is really important to you. Some of what you want, ain't nothin to you. You could let go of the dream and not even miss it.

That's why you got to think 'bout which dreams are true to yo' heart before you start actin' on 'em.

Aine A. Thang

Girl, Ms. Fly ain't got time to waste chasin' fluff. You got a life to fill with come-true dreams.

Since there ain't nothin' to it but to do it, take some time to look back over that list you made up.

Remember to arrange yo' list in them different categories that I told you: money, body, relationships, spirit.

Once you done separate the dreams, then underline the ones that come from the deep. Girl, knowin' yo' deepest desires and movin' toward them, that's the way to make a dollah outta' fifteen cents.

You ain't got to start ahead. Jest finish ahead. Get yo' own tip and stay steady. That's where yo' success lie—livin' life accordin' to what you want and need. Girl, you doin' that and you on the o-fly tip.

A Life of Legacy

As you thinkin' on these things, I want you to realize that what you doin' is makin' a map. You're choosin' where you want yo' life to go. That's why this dream map is one of the most important things you can do in yo' life. Listen up, now. The map ain't important jest 'cause it's a path for helpin' you reach yo' own dreams. It's important 'cause when you movin' on yo' own dreams, then you touchin' other people. You showin' folks somethin'. Makin' yo' life what you want cause you to leave a legacy and a map for other folks.

Ain't nobody got to write no newspaper article on you to make you somebody—'specially not if you got kids. You ain't

Ms. Thang's Guide to Fly

got to read yo' name in *Jet*, or have Oprah do yo' interview. Girl, if yo' life touch jest one other person's life, then you can change the world.

And if you got children, they lookin' to you to know 'bout what they can do in they own lives. That's what legacy all 'bout.

See, you ain't got no room to say that you ain't got nothin' to give nobody. If you ain't got nothin' else, you got dreams for yo'self and yo' children. If somethin' keepin' you from reachin' you dreams, the least you can do is to give yo' children hope that they can reach they dreams.

You know what I'm sayin?

No matter how poor you are, there's one thang ev'rybody can give. You can give hope and heart. You can have faith that yo' kids can do better than what you done.

Faith jest might be the best gift of all.

I know from experience what I'm talkin' 'bout. I lived through some hard days. I remember back when folks was proud to be part of the KKK.

I remember back when Black folks and White folks had separate ev'rythin', even graveyards.

I remember when Black men playin' Step-and-fetch-it was considered fine humor, and lynchin' was somethin' folks did on a Saturday night.

I remember it all, from Ms. Hattie McDaniel acceptin' the first Oscar give out to a Black woman to Mr. Colin Powell bein' the first Black American to be made Secretary of the State.

I seen the wind whippin' and churnin' like to tear my

people apart, and I seen the wind changin' and floatin' my people up to the heavens like they got wings.

Wind ain't change, though, without folks payin' a price for it. There are those who gave ev'rything they had so that my dreams would be easier to reach.

Imagine that.

They might not have even knowed my name, but they wanted better for me. They didn't want me to be judged by my color. They didn't want me to be kept down by my sex.

They worked and suffered to change things that were wrong.

I got to honor that legacy.

I'm aimin' to do my share and leave a legacy, too.

That's the debt I owe to the ones that come befo' me. I raised my babies with that debt. Told my kids straight out, know that the debt to legacy is stronger than any "black tax."

Ev'rybody got some kind of somethin' that can keep 'em back. The debt of legacy is somethin' positive, pushin' you forward.

Girl, talkin' 'bout legacy make me sentimental. I'm gonna' take a moment of silence and think on those women that left a legacy for the rest of us. Ya'll ought to know by now, Ms. Thang got to give respect when it come due.

Ya'll peek my next list. This list got women from the original fly club. Ain't no color scheme to this list. In fact, I tried my best to include women from all races, even tho', as a African American woman, my first thinkin' was to jest write 'bout women of my race. My granddaughter keep tellin' me

Ms. Thang's Guide to Fly

thangs ain't so segregated as they once was. I realize that, of course. Dr. King's crazy dream comin' to be. 'Sides that, I'm livin' here in this nursin' home with all kind of people.

The list ain't in no particular order, neither. All this list show is women with somethin' in they hearts that they thought was worth fightin' for. You might not want to read no list that got to do with givin' respect to the women come befo' you, but, ev'ry woman who want to call herself fly ought to have a role model that did somethin' with her life 'sides hikin' up her dress and lettin' the air hit her in her glory.

These here some women that fought and endured so you young chicks could have life a bit easier than they had. By the way, Ms. Thang sharp enough to know her history, but my granddaughter helped me some on this list an' I thank her for the work she did.

Ms. Thang's Top Ten Fly Divas

Prudence Crandall

Prudence was a White teacher in 1830's Connecticut. She defied the town by allowin' a young Black woman to attend her school for young women. When the other students dropped out, Ms. Crandall opened a school for Colored girls. Ms. Crandall was ignored by the townspeople, but she continued to fight for her students. The school didn't make it. Ms. Crandall was arrested on a trumped up charge. She won her case, but the townpeople set the school on fire and Ms. Fly Crandall had to close down her school for Colored girls.

Sojourner Truth

Used to be called Isabella Baumfree, but Sojourner got herself somethin' to say, and she changed her name so that she could say it. Sojourner didn't care nothin' that she was a former slave. She didn't care that she didn't have no formal education. She didn't care that she didn't have no money. A spiritual woman, she got a call on her life. With nothin' but the clothes on her back and faith, she went 'bout preachin'. Ms. Fly Truth spoke many a time to ignorant people didn't see anythin' but that she was Colored. I read 'bout how some men at one of her speeches claimed she wasn't no woman, but that she was a man. They told her to prove she a woman by undressin' befo' some of the other women that was there. Sojourner got up in front of all of 'em to say she fed many a white baby at her breast, and she would show 'em all the truth of it, 'cause they the ones had somethin' to be shamed for, not her. Sojourner Truth was a strong voice for my people. Ain't many can impress Ms. Thang, but this here one woman make me feel honor jest to be a Black woman.

Marian Wright Edelman

I was 23 years old when this young'un was born. It never stop amazin' me that a woman as young as she was could be 'bout doin' somethin' with her life almost right from the start. Marian was the first Black woman to become a lawyer in Mississippi. She started the Children's Defense Fund and has spent her life workin' for the rights of children and families. Ms. Fly Edelman got a purpose. She once said, "The legacy I want to leave is a childcare system that says no kid is going to be left alone or left unsafe."

Now that's fly.

Marie Curie

The first woman to receive a Nobel prize. Marie Curie was also the first person, not jest woman, to receive a second Nobel prize, and her daughter even got a Nobel prize. Ms. Fly Curie worked on radiation. She came up with the notion of radioactivity. Durin' World War I, they was drivin' little cars 'round the battlefields with Marie Curie's X-ray units on 'em. Women ev'rywhere felt proud 'cause of what this one sister did with her life.

Helen Keller

Like I say, fly ain't 'bout makin' excuses. Helen Keller an example of somebody had ev'ry right to talk 'bout why she couldn't. Left blind, and deaf after a childhood illness, 'stead of makin' excuses, she went to college and graduated at the top of her class. Girlfriend wrote several books and became a champion of civil rights for the blind. It's real easy to find excuses; a body lookin' for an excuse ought not have any trouble findin' one, but Ms. Fly Keller left a legacy that ain't acceptin' no excuses. She original fly.

Elizabeth Cady Stanton

There was many a rally and many a march so that women could express they views in political areas. Elizabeth Cady Stanton fought hard for women to gain the right to vote. Elizabeth was what they call a "suffragette." She started up the first Women's Rights Convention and used what she had learned fightin' slavery. With Susan B. Anthony, Lucretia Mott, Sojourner Truth, and others, Elizabeth Cady Stanton fought for the woman's right to vote. Ya'll know that the Nineteenth Amendment was added to the Constitution on August 26, 1920. Ms. Thang was jest four years old at the time, but even a four-year-old know fly.

Mother Teresa

Ya'll remember Ms. Thang Fly code: Believe, Reach, Achieve, Become, and Teach. Mother Teresa had this down to the bone. Jest like Marian Edleman Wright, Mother Teresa, whose real name was Agnes Gonxha Bojarhiu, spent her entire life helpin' and teachin' others. She was only eighteen years old when she joined with the church. Wasn't long after that, she quit her job as a high-school principal and went to work in India. Folk in this country think they know poor, but Mother Teresa worked with the poorest of poor. She set up a home for the needy and started over 200 charity centers all over the world. She won the Nobel Peace Price in 1979. Mother Teresa beyond fly, so I ain't 'bout to put no label like fly on her. I jest wanna bring her up 'cause she an example to all people that it don't take money to change the world. Changin' the world don't take no count of color. Mother Teresa was Albanian. She didn't let nothin' stop her from livin' the life she wanted to live. Her life made the world a better place. Mother Teresa had heart. Mother Teresa had spirit, and she had it in overflowin' abundance. Another note—Mother Teresa was only six years younger than me. When she died, she was still workin' doin' what she loved to do.

Rosa Parks

Rosa Park is as fly as fly can be. She woke folks up that day in 1955, when she refused to follow that segregation nonsense in Montgomery, Alabama. Ya'll know Ms. Fly Parks ain't never let no one tell her she can't. She was workin' with the NAACP for twelve years before she got arrested in Montgomery. She had a world-changin' attitude. Not only did Ms. Parks change the world that day, she continued workin' to change the world. That's fly.

Aine A. Thang

Ida B. Wells

Ida Wells was a teacher and writer durin' the days of Reconstruction. In fact, she one of the ones that attended the foundin' conference for the NAACP. Like Rosa Parks, Ms. Fly Wells changed the world in many different ways. She was ridin' in a train and some folks objected 'cause she was Black. She refused to move to the smokin' car, so the train conductors carried her out by force. Girlfriend raised a mighty ruckus. Ms. Fly sued the railroad and won. Her bravery made enemies so she started packin' a pistol and jest 'bout dared folks to treat her less than she deserved. She didn't stop there, though. When a good friend of hers got lynched, Ms. Fly Wells put together a record of folks gettin' lynched and what was bein' done (usually nothin') to protect Black folks from these "hate crimes." Her hard work and bravery forced folks to change. Ida also helped organize the National Association of Colored Women. A fighter for her people, Ida Barnett Wells was fly.

Ida B. Wells was at the first meetin' to organize the National Association of Colored Women, but there was another important person at that meetin'. This woman was the oldest person to attend, but she had already been fightin' on the frontlines to help give her people a voice. Her actions durin' the civil war, and the hard times of slavery befo' the civil war, had made her infamous. This woman had been a slave, a cook, and

Ms. Thang's Guide to Fly

a laundress. During the war, she worked as both a nurse, and a spy for the Northern States. As a conductor on the underground railroad, in spite of an injury that caused her to have blackouts, Harriet Tubman still managed to lead over 700 men, women, and children to freedom. At one point, Harriet Tubman had a $40,000 reward on her head. More than fly, Harriet Tubman still serve as a role model to all people in both courage and strength.

Listen up. All kind of folk tryin' to make they mark in the world. Some of 'em tryin' by flashin' they outside assets, some of 'em developin' they inside assets. Girl, don't you know that it's them inside assets that spill out. Inside assets show up on yo' face. They make up who you are. Ms. Wanna-be fly, you got to know that them inside assets touch other lives, even to the next generation.

Let it be for the good.

CANE SENSE:

- Havin' the right attitude a foundation of fly.

- Folks don't judge you by the fact that you are, they judge you by what you do with who you are.

- Passin' on to those who come after you, whether it's yo' own children or another adult, is like givin' a gift that get stronger with each generation.

Ms. Thang Speaks

On Purpose Fly

CHAPTER 9
▼

On Purpose Fly

> While you busy apin' the latest five-minute star,
> yo' life movin' on and you ain't doin' nothin'
> with what you got that make you you.

These days, folks so busy lookin' at what somebody else got, they can't see what they got in they own hands.

Folks wantin' to be somebody they ain't—somebody that got it like that.

While you busy apin' the latest five-minute star, yo' life movin' on and you ain't doin' nothin' with what you got that make you you.

Now, ain't nothin' wrong with lookin' up to folks that got talent, but you got to do yo' own thing.

Fly ain't 'bout apin' nobody. Fly 'bout individual skills. This here yo' time to be selfish right. When you tryin' to develop yo' skills, when you lookin' to the future of yo' life, that's all you developin' yo'self. Other folks ain't got the right to tell you who you ought to be, other than expectin' you to be a decent human bein'. Yo' life is yo' life.

Too many folks ain't got no idea 'bout who they want to be

or what they want to do. Like I say befo' I ain't 'bout to tell you who to be.

But I can tell you what I do.

New Year come 'round, 'stead of makin' resolutions, I decide where I wanna' go skills-wise. I don't care what no million-dollar-suit-wearin' motivational speaker tell you, life ain't jest 'bout makin' money. It's 'bout bein' the money.

Them skills you got attract money and set you on the path to bein' able to get to yo' dreams.

If yo' dream is to travel, get a job in the travel industry. Work in a company that send you places, or make enough money to go where you wanna' go. Those are yo' choices. Either that, or don't go nowhere.

Ya'll hear what I'm sayin'?

Folks runnin' 'round tryin' to figure out ways to get money. That ain't the way it work. You ain't got to find a way. You got to be the way. It's all 'bout yo' skills. People pay cold, hard cash for skills.

I don't know 'bout you, but I always did like havin' cold, hard cash. Kinda' made me feel warm inside, when I knew I could pay my bills. Don't listen to nobody tellin' you that you got to be poor to be happy and holy.

Please. Bein' rich ain't make you happy by itself and bein' poor ain't make you happy. The fly way is to get skills doin' what you love. You attractin' money doin' what you love, then, girl, you bound to attract happy, too.

If you ain't got no skills that you tryin' to develop, you jest treadin' water, waitin' to die, or somethin', I don't know.

Ms. Thang's Guide to Fly

What I do know is that if you ain't developin' yo'self, then don't be lookin' for a hand up, 'cause you workin' from a hand-out mentality.

It's time for me to talk to my people. Black folk, more than anybody else, hate steppin' outside they comfort zone.

I get so sick of Black people talkin' 'bout what Black folk can and can't do. Seem like the list of can'ts longer than the list of cans.

And Lord help us all if somebody get above herself enough to think she can do somethin' ain't no other Black folks doin'.

Can somebody please tell me what kind of thinkin' is that? Ain't fly thinkin'.

If you thinkin' like that, then I know you ain't got the nerve to complain 'bout how they ain't got no Black folk doin' this, that, and the other.

That's jest plain crazy.

Who's gonna' break barriers if it ain't you?

Learn somethin', girl. Don't matter if what you learnin' new to you, long as you got an interest in it. And don't let fear stop you.

I heard tell this story 'bout how some prisoners were given the choosin' of the way they want to die. They could die by hangin', or they could go through this large, black door, and face whatever on the other side.

Ev'ry one of them prisoners chose hangin' over the black door. Later on, somebody asked what it was behind the door that had the prisoners too scared to pick it. "Ain't nothin behind that door but freedom," says the law man. It's jest that most folks don't know what to do with freedom. Hangin' they know, and that's why they chose it. They want what they understand, not what they don't.

Can't recall who told that story, prob'bly one of them infomercials sellin' soap, or a way to get thin, but the story stayed with me.

Ev'rytime I do my Ms. Fly Skills plannin', I try to add somethin' new, somethin' that I don't know a whole lot 'bout. And I think 'bout that story of them people choosin' the hangin' over somethin' they don't know.

A lot of folk do anythin' they can to avoid learnin' somethin' new. To my way of thinkin' that's jest foolish. I can stay with what I know, or I can go with that big black door. The other side of that door might be failure or freedom, but I won't know if I don't open the door.

If I find freedom on the other side, then I'm doubly blessed. If I find failure, then I'm 'bout to learn somethin'.

Now I know that failure ain't s'posed to be an option. Maybe it ain't an option in war. It ain't an option in a love story or a fiction book, but in real life, real folks failin' ev'ry day. The smart ones get up. They dust theyselves off. They keep steppin'. The ones thinkin' hoochie give up. They complain. They look for excuses so they can lay where they fall.

Fall I may, many times, but success a part of my race. Success a part of my gender.

Been awhile since I give a top ten list. Since we talkin' skills, I got the Top Ten career choices for Hoochies.

Ms. Thang's Guide to Fly

Top Ten Hoochie Career Opportunities

1. Throwin' down with white-bread Hollywood actors lookin' for a cheap lay with a touch of exotic

2. Throwin' down with the sleezoid jerk boss aka harass-em-Harry, who can't get NONE of that funky stuff from nobody else

3. Talk show guest on the loser show

4. Punchin' bag

5. Gang-banger hottie

6. Lock-up princess

7. Cover queen for some sensational news rag for at least fifteen minutes

8. Well-known actress, for at least fifteen minutes, if not less

9. The town hoochie—Yeah, folks still talk 'bout you if you fass and nasty.

10. Ain't-never-gettin'-there wannabe

Aine A. Thang

Some folks say bein' a hoochie a fine career choice. Only problem with that is the folks doin' the sayin' are usually married men ain't worth nothin' to they wives and out creepin' for hoochies to satisfy they nasty itch.

They ain't thinkin' 'bout you. Girl, they thinkin' 'bout that itch. Some of 'em messed up enough that if you ain't scratchin' they itch, they jest as soon find a baboon to scratch it.

One mo once, girl, yo' life is yourn. You ain't on the planet 'cause you got fingernails long enough to hit all the right places. Let Ms. Thang break this down quick.

You are on the planet with a purpose.

Jest make good sense that if you on the planet with a purpose, then you should apply yo'self to findin' out what that purpose is. Can't be happy livin' down below what you got inside for the rest of yo' life. Livin' below somethin' you do when you ain't got no other choice. Livin' yo' life to the fullest potential inside you is what make a body happy. That's where yo' joy is.

Maybe you don't know what I mean by purpose. Jest like misunderstandin' discipline, folks been misunderstandin' purpose since befo' time began. I already spoke on 'bout how discipline is doin' what you need to do when you need do it. Well, purpose is kin to that. Purpose is 'bout knowin' who you are.

I know this all mixed up, but I'll be makin' things clear in a bit. First, get this knowledge in yo' brain.

Ms. Thang's Guide to Fly

What's Purpose?

When you know who you are, the knowin' will help you make the choice on how to spend yo' time.

When you know yo' purpose, the knowin' will help you choose doin' what's right for you.

Look at it like this. Some folks made to play sports, some ain't. Some folks made to sing, some ain't.

Some folks you can't tell nothin' 'bout, then all the sudden, they break open with all kind of gifts.

They surprise you.

Sometimes, they surprise theyselves.

That's purpose. And glory, ain't no one purpose better than any other purpose. Long as you ain't hurtin' nobody, then it's all good.

When you tryin' to understand yo' purpose, make sure you know that purpose is 'bout what's inside of you—not 'bout gettin' rich.

Too many folks chasin' money thangs, thinkin' if they play hoops they makin' good roads.

Maybe they are. Many a man raised the standards for hisself and his own thataway, but gettin' rich ain't no purpose.

Once you rich, then what?

Chasin' money ain't no purpose.

Remember what I said earlier? Be the money, and the money will come. But rich ain't jest 'bout money. Rich got to do with fulfillin' yo' purpose, havin' yo' needs met, both body and soul.

Aine A. Thang

That's rich. Ev'rything on top jest gravy.

That's the danger of folks bein' so busy tryin' to make money. They ain't willin' to push through to they purpose, and they endin up doin' stuff they was never meant to do, all for the sake of gettin' g'd up.

Hear me right, now. Ain't nothin' wrong with money. Money a good thang. If you ain't got it, you know I'm right.

Money ain't the problem, it's folks chasin' money. Ain't nothin' like chasin' money to make a body miserable.

Ain't nothin' like chasin' money make it disappear.

Advertisin' folks got somethin' they call "push–pull". A pushin' ad tellin' you how you got to get the product and maybe even tellin' you to call now. A pull ad don't tell you to buy. It jest showin' you folks happy with the product, like somebody drinkin' coffee and the sun start shinin' on them. Know what I'm sayin'?

The ad ain't tellin' you that the sun will shine on you if you drink coffee. The ad tellin' you that if you drink they coffee, you will feel like the sun is shinin' on you.

You believe that; and, without anybody even tellin' you, you go out and buy Aine-Nuthin'-But-Caffeine coffee.

You weren't pushed. You were pulled by a picture of what you wanted yo' life to look like.

The sun might or might'nt shine when you drinkin' that coffee, but it don't matter. Yo' mind has the picture of the ad in it. And when you drinkin' that coffee, you see yo'self as bein' like the person in the ad.

Then you feel good.

Ms. Thang's Guide to Fly

Same thang happen with purpose.

You can live yo' life pushin' yo'self at somethin' ain't got nothin' to do with who you supposed to be. On the deep side, you know that you ain't livin' like you want, but you pushin' outside of yo' purpose cause you think that's the only way for you to get the wherewithal you need to survive.

The other side of that is the pullin' side. When you workin' accordin' to who you are then, like rain in the Spring, you gonna' be feedin' others and feedin' yo'self. Rain in the Spring is valuable. Folks prayin' for it. They want it. They need it. They'd pay good money to get it comin' they way.

That's what pull is.

Pullin' make money come to you on its own feet. From yo' point of view, it ain't work. You bein' who you are. You deliverin' the good inside of you, the good in yo' nature. That's why, if you truly want to be fly, you got to get with yo' purpose.

Know who you are.

Black Grandma Talkin', now, listen up. Ms. Thang got fly down cold, but befo' you go tryin' to scare up a purpose, I jest want to remind you 'bout a few thangs.

1. Can't no one tell you who you are, not even me, and Ms. Thang the diva of direction.

2. Purpose ain't comin' from outside you. It's already inside you. It's somethin' you know down low in yo' gut.

3. You need to know yo' purpose to move toward it.

One of the best thangs 'bout bein' old is that I spend my time fillin' up with good knowledge, so I'm 'bout to deliver some road maps.

I can't say what yo' destination is, but I can give you a map that show some ways to gettin' where you want to go.

Gettin' there up to you.

Ms. Thang's Road Map to Purpose

Ain't all that difficult findin' yo purpose. The hard part is followin' yo' dream. The hard part is bein' honest 'bout who you are and what you really want.

The first thang you need to do to figure purpose is to take a clock minute an' think on what you like to do. Think on what you enjoy. What gets you off the sofa and doin' with a happy heart? What you wish you was doin' right now?

Next, think 'bout the things that come easy for you: You a songbird, can holla' like nobody business? Can you can paint pictures more beautiful than Da Vinci?

What you got inside of you, girl? We 'bout to do some diggin' and bring it out.

Comin' up, I got Ms. Thang's Purpose Profile. It's time to commit to yo'self. And keep in mind, we thinkin' like Ms. Fly now. Don't want no hoochie thinkin' on this list. This list got to do with creatin', bringin' the good from inside to the out.

Ms. Thang's Guide to Fly

Purpose Profile

　　Butcher, baker, candlestick maker . . . what you want to be? It's a sad fact of life that we don't always get to chose what we want to do as our day job; but that don't mean you shouldn't be developin' yo' skills. And you ain't got to spend yo' life doin' the same thing. If you want to be a butcher and a baker and candlestick maker, then be all that. Be all that you can be, Ms. Girl.

　　If you got skills here, there, and ev'rywhere, then can't nobody stick you in a rut 'cause you always got somethin' else you can do with yo'self. You develop yo'self, then, when the time come for you to show what you know, you gonna' deliver better than Pizza Hut, 'cause you'll have the goods.

Aine A. Thang

PURPOSE PROFILE

First step in movin' toward yo' fly is to know what it is inside you that make you who you are. I got the goods to get you started. Check out "Ms. Thang Purpose Profile."

My name:

My age:

Where I got my start:

What I got goin' on right now:

Ms. Thang's Guide to Fly

Where I want to be next year:
    Spirit-wise:

    Money-wise:

    Body-wise:

Aine A. Thang

Career-wise:

Relationship-wise:

My strengths:

Ms. Thang's Guide to Fly

What I got to change:

What I got to learn:

Where I'm 'bout to start:

Aine A. Thang

Ms. Thang Purpose Profile

My name: Aine A. Thang, aka, Granny Fly

My age: You do not have to answer this question, girl. Who put this in here? I didn't authorize this question! Hmph! Folks always tryin' to nose out somebody's age. Ms. Fly is ageless, baby.

Where I got my start:

When my granddaughter, Ms. Sidditty, came to me to talk 'bout how she was tryin' to help some young'uns, I told her my opinion. She thought we ought to make a book out of it. Before that, I got my start in Georgia, small town name of Elfrida.

What I got goin' on right now:

Gettin' ready to start the next book. I've had my say to the women, now it's time to break it down for the men.

Where I want to be next year:

Spirit-wise: Girl, Granny Fly will still be givin' glory to the Creator. That's my world view, would like to make it to church a little more often, though.

Ms. Thang's Guide to Fly

Money-wise:

Wouldn't hurt to be rollin' in greenbacks, although, at my age, rollin' might be a little on the hard side. Ain't got much purpose for money at this point in life—other than to leave somethin' behind for my family and a charity or two. But, really, this here question need a specific answer. I want to earn $50,000 next year on appearances and endorsements. Hear that, Centrum Silver? Heck, I'll endorse Phillips Milk of Magnesia. . . . Hmm, maybe I should write a book 'bout all the different thangs you can do with the stuff in that big blue bottle.

Body-wise:

Be nice to be able to jump outta' bed in the mornings, instead of creak out. Yeah, I'm 'bout to pick me up some of them Tae-bo tapes ev'rybody talkin' 'bout. Might as well start weight-liftin', too. I want the body of a fifty year old. I wanna' hear folks say, "Don't mess with Granny Fly, that old lady can kick butt!"

Career-wise:

All I got to say right here is, Steven Spielberg, call me. We'll do lunch, Shug. It's time to look past *E.T.* and *The Color Purple* (Go, Alice, go, Alice). Granny Fly got yo' entertainment vehicle right c'here. Like I said befo', call me, boy, cause I still got my driver's license. I'll come see you, if you want.

Relationship-wise:

I have been blessed in my relationships. Only ever was one man for me—Spencer. Spencer been gone for awhile now, and I ain't lookin' to replace him. I'm jest thankful and grateful that I got kids and grandkids, and even great-grandkids, who care 'bout me. That didn't come 'bout cause of blood. That came 'bout cause of me carin' for them. Lord, jest help me stay in my right mind so I know the folks that come to see me.

My strengths:

I love to work with my hands. I crochet, knit, and sew. I earned me a bit of money, too, sellin' my work at craft fairs and the like. And I'm real proud that I passed that love of workin' with my hands on to my young'uns come after me. Most all my kids can sew. One daughter is a interior designer, another one does graphic art.

On occasion, I have been known to make up some of the best peach pie this side of Glory. Did I mention that my son own his own restaurant? That's my buttered peach pie recipe on the menu over at Eddie T's.

Proud Momma talkin', now: My children took things that I taught them—things that they loved to do, too—and added they own special fire to move they lives ahead.

Some folks call it a circle. My Momma and my Granny

Ms. Thang's Guide to Fly

taught me how to sew and knit and crochet, and I always tell my children that they come from a long line of craftin' peoples. That gives them somethin' to look to, a legacy to pass on to they children, and now, they children's children.

Sure there was times my kids didn't seem to be listenin'. Didn't matter. I kept speakin' to them on who they was and should be. I never pressed nothin' on 'em—like tellin' 'em they had to be doctors or lawyers. That there is they decision—but I let those kids know if they good enough for God's purpose, don't matter none what nobody else have to say 'bout 'em.

Ain't no excuses in fly.

Many a time my kids have said that they glad I let them know they history.

What I got to change:

Not one thang, girl. I am happy. Although, I'm thinkin' 'bout relocating to one of them Eden-type nursin' homes—the ones where they bring in kids and dogs and stuff. Might be fun. I'll let you know.

What I got to learn:

Now that I'm writin' books, I might go on back to school and brush up on standard English. I come from a time when we didn't even have separate but equal. Tryin' to learn somethin' was a lynchin' matter. Still, even though I have opportunity, I don't know whether speakin' different is somethin' I want or need to do. Sometimes, you jest got to say thangs the way they mean somethin' to you. I like my slangy-way. Course, slangy don't set too well with the chi-chi folks, but if it ain't impedin', then I ain't needin'. Ya'll need to let me know on this one. If my slang is too much for yo' generation, then I ain't afraid of applyin' myself to learn. I had to put some work in on updatin' my be-bop rap to hip-hop. It was fun, learnin' the new slang. 'Sides, ain't nobody too old to learn. You too old to learn, then you might as well pick out that plot at the graveyard, cause that's where you belong.

Where I'm 'bout to start:

Thing I'm focused on is the next book. That's where I got my goals set. So, that's where I'm 'bout to start. Almost ev'ry book, even books that give opinion, start with research. I got to do some research on what's appropriate for men in this generation. Then, I'll give my opinion on the rights and the wrongs.

My Own Personal Fly

You may not think much of my list, and that's yo' right. but, I filled out the profile to give you an example to go by. You start with the dreams and then the profile to show you where you should be settin' your goals.
The dream map and the profile teach you 'bout who you really are.

Ms. Thang's Guide to Fly

See, the things I love make me who I am. That's what keepin' it real mean. Keepin' real to Ms. Thang. If Ms. Thang got a dream of movin' up to the East Side, West Side, rich side, Eden-style nursin' home, whatever, then I ain't keepin' it real stayin' on the down side, am I? I'm jest denyin' the real.

Mick ears, now: There ain't no Ms. Thang without that dream map and profile. It's all 'bout me. If there is a Ms. Thang, she Ms. Thang, Junior, somebody else, not me.

My dreams help me make my place in the world.

My understanding of self, girl, that's what help me connect to other people in a good way.

And, 'cause Ms. Thang got herself together and know where she at, I been able to pass on to my children.

I spent my life teachin' my own children that they a gift to this world. They got something inside them; somethin' inside to give to they neighborhood, to they church, to the lives of other folks.

It's that debt we talked 'bout earlier. That debt say that we take what we need, and we pass on from our abundance. Passin' on is jest as important as the takin'.

Oprah Winfrey say her success wouldn't have been, if not for the ones that came before her.

I didn't quote Ms. Fly Winfrey right, but the spirit of what she said is there. I agree with her. That's why I worked so hard to raise my kids with a fly mindset. That's why I'm puttin' out what I know 'bout fly in a book. When I leave this place, I want to leave with the peace in my heart of knowin' I tried my best to live a life that used my talents and gave back to other folks.

That's what I want. That's my drivin' purpose; but, my purpose ain't your purpose. That's why you got to look inside yo'self to fill out the purpose profile. You got to know yo' own personal fly. Ain't nothin' hard to it. Jest be honest.

You need to take a look at yo' dream map and that profile at least once a week. Keep remindin' yo'self of things that are important to you. These two things will be where we get the goods to set yo' personal fly goals.

Before we set goals, though, we got to go back to dealin' with the mind.

Purpose and Discipline

Before you filled out yo' profile, we talked 'bout two of the most important thangs that make up fly: Discipline and Purpose. Less'n we forget, here go the breakdown:

1. Discipline got you doin' what need to be done when it need to be done.

2. Purpose lettin' you know who you are so you can decide what need to be done.

One mo' word 'bout purpose. When you got purpose, you openin' the door to a joy so deep and pure, you won't be needin' to drown no sorrows in drugs and alcohol. Try it and see. I ain't tryin' to make no promises I can't keep. You find yo' purpose,

Ms. Thang's Guide to Fly

and you'll find yo' measure of happiness.

Like I already say, dreamin' the easy part. Easy as Ms. Thang slappin' my gums together 'bout purpose. But livin' out a life of purpose ain't always easy. Keep that in mind. That's why true fly ain't 'bout wardrobe. What you put on yo'self is a reflection of what you got goin' on inside yo' mind.

If I had a choir standin' up behind me, I'd make 'em sing Hallelujah right now. Hallelujah! Hallelujah! The inside will always find a way to show up on yo' outside.

That's why you got to check yo'self. Once you understand who you are, you on the way to creatin' somethin'. It jest might be that creatin' somethin', movin' forward to yo' dreams is a new thang for you. If that's the case, you got to make sure you done already dealt with the mind, cause girl, on the path to fly, you will have issues. Ms. Thang here to testify. If you want to reach yo' dreams, you gonna' have to move, and issues are jest part of movement.

Think on it this way: fly don't come without tests.

When you in school, the teacher give you tests. There're three reasons a good teacher give a test:

1. So the teacher can know what you know.

2. So the teacher can know what you don't know.

3. So the teacher can let you know what you need to work on.

A i n e   A .   T h a n g

Now, I ain't got no test to give you. Ain't no need for me to go testin' you. Life create its own tests. When you strivin' to reach fly, you pass some tests, you fail others. When you a hoochie, a lot of what you facin' is Consequences.

All I can do for you is drop some knowledge 'bout the tests you gonna' have to pass to get to fly.

So, Mick ears, girl, three things: to be fly, you got to be disciplined.

You got to understand yo' purpose and know yo'self.

You got to know how to deal with the mind and deal with issues that come up on the path to fly. Don't matter whether you call 'em life tests or issues, if you can deal with 'em, then girl, can't nobody stop you.

Now, Ms. Thang can't tell you how to deal, but I can clue you 'bout some of the issues.

Time for another Ms. Thang top ten.

Ms. Thang's Top Nine Purpose Issues

1. Wrong attitude

Now it jest goes without my sayin', you ain't 'bout to deliver the goods if you ain't got the deliverin' attitude. Folks always want to make a problem somebody else's fault, but right here is where most problems start. If yo' attitude ain't fly, then you ain't 'bout to be.

Ms. Thang's Guide to Fly

Fly Attitude Profile:

You ready to do what needs doin'.

You ain't lookin' for no problems to jump into.

A problem come along, you there with the solution, 'cause that's what you are, a problem-solvin' sister.

You doin' what needs doin' the right way.

If you don't know how, you find out.

That's the fly attitude you want to profile. You go showin' that kind of face, and you gonna' be breakin' down walls you ain't even seen yet. Too many folks, Black, White, and Alien-Green, got problem attitudes. You change yours up, even jest a little, and watch the doors open up to you.

2. Wrong friends

What the Good Book say 'bout wrong friends? Bad friends one thing, wrong friends another. Bad friends lead you on the path of destruction. Wrong friends ain't leadin' nowhere, ain't goin' nowhere, don't want you goin' nowhere. It's jest human to want to fit in with our friends. You start tryin' to do somethin' positive with yo' life and got the wrong kind of friends, they ain't 'bout to become yo' cheerin' section. The problem is that when you start movin' and doin', it make them feel uncomfortable. Yo' dream-reachin' make them look at theyselves, and if they don't like what they see, they ain't like to blame theyselves. They might jest blame you. Hardest thang in the world is changin' friends, but if that's what you got to do, then that's what you got to do. If you can bring somebody along with you, fine and good, but if they don't want to come, let 'em alone and come on yo' own.

3. Lack of plan

Ain't no firm foundation built without a plan. Some people keep plans in they mind, others write 'em out and study them like the Word. I think writin' 'em down is best. You write it down, you won't forget nothin'.

4. Lack of knowledge

Ain't no shame in a lack of knowledge. Jest 'cause you don't know, don't mean you can't know. It ain't hard to learn how to do. Once you decide yo' interests, learnin' jest the next step. Ain't nothin' hard 'bout learnin' when you learnin' what you want and need. If you ain't got the money to take a class, then the library can be your new place to hang. If you live in a city with a lot of 'burbs, visit ev'ry one of the libraries 'round. 'Burb libraries don't carry the whole of what's been ordered. They divide the books up, and you have to go 'round and get to know who got what. Make sure you responsible, too. Ain't no sense in not bein' able to check out books 'cause you ain't been returnin' 'em. Don't ask nobody 'bout Ms. Thang in this area. I still got some books to return.

5. Lack of understandin'

Gettin' knowledge is the easy part. Gettin' understandin', now that's hard. A lot of folk thinkin' they somethin' 'cause of what they know, but while they knowin' a lot, they ain't got no understandin'. They don't know nothin' 'bout usin' what they know, or why they should use what they know. You can have discipline. You can have yo' purpose down cold. You can have yo' knowledge, but if you ain't got the understandin' 'bout why, then you ain't got understandin'. Let me say that again.

Understandin' tellin' you the why of yo' talents.

Let me break it down this way:

Purpose tellin' you what
Knowledge sayin' how
Discipline sayin' when and where
Understandin' got yo' why.

6. Lack of focus

When you got yo' purpose set, the last thing you needin' to do is listen to a lot of hoo-rah 'bout how sister so-and-so did this and that, and if you lookin' to make yo' road good, then you need to drop that thang you doin' and come on over here. When you get yo' purpose set, don't be double-minded. Double-minded woman unstable in all her ways. Focus on yo' purpose plan and keep movin' on the path you set for yo'self. Other folks can do what they gonna' do. You doin' for you. You ain't sister so-and-so; you ain't gettin' judged on how well you lived her life. You gettin' judged on what you did in yo' life.

Now, I ain't tellin' you to stick on no blinders so you can't see what's happenin' around you. Focus mean keepin' yo' eye on yo' goal, and sayin' "no" to what don't fit with what you decided you wanted to be. Jest like you can make a choice 'bout doin' drugs or not, you choose the person you are. You choose. Each day, you choose by what you do, what you thinkin' on, and what you puttin' yo' attention on.

Choose to put yo' attention on what you need for each step in reachin' yo' goals. That's focus.

7. Lack of confidence

Lack of confidence come from three things: One, lack of knowledge; two, lack of experience; three, fear.

We done talked 'bout gettin' knowledge. Studyin' up on what you interested in ain't nothin' but a thang.

Lackin' experience ain't too difficult to overcome, neither. Ev'rythang you do can be put on yo' resume, even if you ain't got paid for it. That's what Miss Ann kin tellin' her. Volunteer, it look good on yo' resume. Befo' you roll yo' eyes at the idea of tradin' yo' talent for a line on yo' resume, think 'bout it. I say,

Ms. Thang's Guide to Fly

it's better to trade time for learnin', than to waste time an' never learn.

I never did go to the Tuskegee Normal and Industrial Institute, as it was called back in the day, but it was, far as I know, the first place where folks was taught learnin' by doin'. Now, learnin' by doin' a buzz phrase. At Tuskegee, they didn't jest get book learnin', they went to workin' in the fields they was studyin'.

Booker T. was on to somethin' with that idea. You want to hone yo' talent? Practice and then practice some more. If you can't find nobody to pay you while you learnin', then find someone to let you work for free to get the skills you need. Don't look for no excuses for not gettin' experience, 'cause somebody somewhere lookin' for what you can provide.

Now, what you s'posed to do if you ain't got no belief in yo'self, if you afraid you can't make the grade? I ain't 'bout to touch on why you think the way you do. I'll leave all that to the talk shows, but, if Rikki Lake can figure out the answer to yo' problem in an hour talk show, then why you been wastin' years wonderin' what was wrong with you?

If you don't trust yo'self because you a flake, then change yo' behavior. Start out practicin' makin' different choices. In her book, *Steppin' Out With Attitude*, Anita Bunkley wrote 'bout ten thangs you need to work so that folks will think positively 'bout you.

Anita's list good and ev'rythin', but I got to drop her words in Ms. Thang vernacular.

Aine A. Thang

Be easy-goin'

Think 'bout other folks

Don't start none, so that there won't be none

Ain't no reason to be rude

Deliver the goods and do it right

Don't go runnin' yo' mouth and tellin' ev'rything you know

Get yo' stuff done without a lot of hoo-rah and bother

Don't play favorites

Tell the truth with love in yo' heart

When you givin', give out of the overflow in yo' heart

If you live like that, you ain't got no cause to be afraid of nobody.

8. Lack of support

There's times a body got to stand alone for a bit before other folk start believin'. For a lot of folk, that's the hardest time. That's when it's temptin' to give up. I been tryin' to encourage you to think fly and let yo' dreams guide you to success, but I'm gonna' step back now, let my fly sister, Ms. Ella Fitzgerald, speak to you on that. Ms. Ella knew hard times, tryin' to make it back in the day when didn't matter how much talent you had, doors were still closed to you on account of color. Ms. Ella was comin' from a place of understandin' when she said, "Don't give up tryin' to do what you really want to do."

See, it don't matter if other folks 'round you don't ever believe in the good dream you got. You might be whilin' with the wrong crowd. Ain't no call for actin' boojee, but Ms. Young Fly got to know that her crew an influence on her. You hang with drug fiends, be careful, less you become that thing. You hang with hoochies, be careful, befo' too long . . . you know what I'm sayin'? Sometime Ms. Fly got to know how to be without a posse. If yourn ain't doin' nothin' but pullin' you down, be brave enough to pull out. That's why it take courage to be fly. That's why fly ain't 'bout what you wearin' today an' tomorrow. This here where the rubber meet the pavement. To be fly, you got to choose who your friends are.

Choosin' Friends

Ms. Thang ain't sayin' choose yo' friends based on money or success. That's on the shallow side. All I'm sayin' is take care in who you lettin' influence you, an' be aware that the folks you whilin' with will influence you.

Aine A. Thang

Pick yo' friends this way:

➙ *They got your back.* You know that you know you can trust 'em. Ain't no way to know that 'til they proved theyselves, so don't go givin' trust up 'til you know who you givin' trust to. Trust mean you can trust 'em with yo' money, yo' man, an' yo' business. Mick ears, girl, friends ain't showin' up on Jenny talkin' 'bout how you got to change this, that, or the other. True, now.

Yo' friend can't come to you in private to lay out yo' private business? Somebody pull you on a talk show to rap 'bout how you got to change, that body only tryin' to earn some notoriety.

➙ *They ain't killin' what you tryin' to grow.* Ain't nothin' worse than havin' a friend that shoot down all yo' dreams. Now you got to be careful to know the difference between good advice an' bad advice. A good friend will let you know 'bout that piece of toilet paper flappin' in the breeze from yo' backside. A good friend will let you know if yo' man is creepin'. A good friend will tell you the truth. A good friend won't tell you that you can't. Sometime it's hard to know a person's motivation. If yo' friend always tryin' to hold you back, always tryin' to get you to do things her way, then you think long an' hard 'bout whether she a true friend, or not.

➙ *She got faith in you.* She got faith in what you can do. A woman need friends, good friends; an', glory, good friends

Ms. Thang's Guide to Fly

hard to come by. But it's yo' good friends keep you goin' when you ain't got no idea how you gonna' put one foot in front of the other. A true friend know you an' believe in you, even when you can't believe in yo'self.

Awright. I got to get back to the issues. But one mo' word on faith. Yo' friend can have faith in you, but 'less you got faith in yo'self, you still ain't likely to go nowhere. Don't ya'll know that befo' Madam C.J. Walker, all a woman had to go on was what she had inside herself? Come on, now. 8-G, it's time for this generation of women to join up with the IFWC. Get yo' card, Baby Girl Fly.

Look, you ain't got no reason to doubt yo'self an' what you can do when you usin' yo' fly tool kit. Each one of us come to life with our own personal fly kit. God put three things in yo' kit an' yo' job is to use those things to get somewhere with yo' life.

Yo' Personal Fly Kit

- You got a brain. Girl, don't you know yo' brain is a muscle? You got to use it, or lose it. Work that thing. Make it buff as a Chippendale dancer.

- God also gave you a body. Ya'll ever heard of Joni Eareckson Tada? This woman had her neck broke in an accident. In spite of the fact that she paralyzed from the neck down, she's an artist. Since she can't use her hands, she use her mouth to move the brush across the canvas. As God is my secret judge, I don't know how any woman of able body can complain 'bout this an' that bein' a handicap. An' claimin' that race a handicap. . . maybe it is, maybe it ain't. Maybe it's only a handicap to the body that's thinkin' it's a handicap. I don't want my color any other way, an' I come up when color mean more than it mean these days. You young'uns livin' in an age where, for ev'ry evil-eye bigot, you got two or three folk don't see nothin' but what you do with yo' life. I ain't sayin' there ain't no dividedness. There divideness aplenty. There prejudice aplenty. Some of it our fault, some of other folks' fault. Some of it jest life. All I'm tryin' to say is that you can't let none of all that stop you.

Fly, broke down to bottom-line essence, simply mean that you got the ability to deliver somethin' got value. Ms. Fly showin' an' provin'. To show and prove, girl you got to know what you capable of. If you ain't know who you are, then you got the problem, it ain't yo' color. You can look good enough to put up on the cover of *Essence* magazine but, girl, if you ain't got the goods on the inside, then none of that like to continue. Ms. Thang got the last word on this here issue. Know yo' value (ain't nobody talkin' 'bout bein' high-brow. I mean know yo' abilities), an' steady deliver on time, an' time after time. Color—whatever color you are— ain't nothin' but a badge. I'm 'bout to drop some science now. Folks in the know lookin' to explain color

Ms. Thang's Guide to Fly

been studyin' up on it, an' they ain't know for sure, but they thinkin' color really do got to do with how much sun yo' ancestors had to deal with. I don't claim to know. Fact is, don't nobody know. But if what they sayin' true, then ain't no such thing as a difference between you an' them people tryin' to claim they superior, 'cept for culture an' beliefs. Ya'll know they looked at all our genes an' found ain't no difference 'cept for one little piece that come from yo' momma an' daddy, an' that piece ain't got nothin' to do with nothin' except for hair color, eye color an' the stuff they call color—melanin. Melanin ain't nothin' but a bit of extra color come from yo' ancestors to protect you from the hot African sun. Don't mean you ain't got the goods. Ev'rybody born with the same kit. Be smart usin' yours.

☞ Last thang God give you to make yo' way in this world is a fightin' spirit. Ain't nothin' come so easy that you ain't got to fight for it. Most of the time, the one you need to fight is yo'self:

Fight laziness.
Fight insecurity.
Fight all them issues that keep you from bein' fly.

Most want to fight other folk. While they fightin' the wrong battles, life goin' on. By the time you get done fightin' other people, you liable to be too old to win the war. Fight people last. Fight yo'self first. When you got yo' discipline, yo' purpose, yo' knowledge an' yo' issues worked out, then you can look 'round an' see who standin' in yo' way. Chances are, ain't nobody froggy enough to jump in yo' path, not as tough as you are. Somebody fool enough to try an' mess with Ms. Fly jest providin' frog legs for dinner.

We only got one final issue to talk 'bout, but it's one of the most important issues:

9. Misuse of purpose

> Ain't no sight more sad than somebody mis-usin' they purpose. See it all the time in church circles, Somebody get a little bit of the Glory of God on him, an' he try to use that talent for makin' hisself rich. Somebody got a talent for singin', they get so caught up in who they thinkin' they are, that they forget who they called to be.

How can you tell if you misusin' yo' purpose?

Well, girl, you got to know 'bout purpose. Purpose ain't got nothin' to do with tryin' to be fly, or tryin' to get folks to ooh an' ahh over you. That's girlish thinkin'. When I'm callin' you girl, I hope ya'll know Ms. Thang usin' courtesy. The aim of this here book to encourage you to become a fly woman.

Ms. Thang's Guide to Fly

Ain't nobody dealin' in little girl fairy tales here. You tryin' to reach real dreams—dreams that might got started when you was little, an' now you on the path. Ms. Thang got two ways to check yo'self, see if you misusin' yo' purpose.

1. You misusin' yo' purpose if yo' purpose only good for you an' nobody else. Since you ain't like to get to yo' dreams all on yo' own, then you got to bring somethin' of value with you in yo' dealin's with other folk. That mean yo' purpose got to touch other folks with good.

2. You misusin' yo' purpose if you ain't leavin' a clear path for somebody else to follow an' find they way. I call it leavin' a legacy on the planet. When you get to where you tryin' to go, you need to turn 'round an' pull somebody else up. Mentorin', they call it these days. Teachin', I call it. Teach somebody else. Encourage somebody else.

   Now, don't cast yo' pearls befo' swine. Make sure the folks you mentorin' got that fly attitude down, otherwise, you can spend all yo' time helpin' somebody only to have them fail, then turn 'round an' blame you. Teachin' help you leave a legacy. Keep in mind, they only two types of legacy: One for the bad an' the other for good. Which one you leave up to you.

Aine A. Thang

CANE SENSE

- Fly ain't 'bout apin' nobody. Fly 'bout individual skills.
- You got the choice to develop yo' skills.
- You on the planet with a purpose.
- You the only one can decide yo' purpose.
- There will be issues in achievin' yo' purpose.

Ms. Thang Speaks

360-Degree Fly

CHAPTER 10

▼

360-Degree Fly

*My wish is that you got smooth roads
all the way through yo' journey.*

We done covered discipline, purpose, issues an' ev'ry bit of ground betwixt an' between fly, so now it's time to get 360-Degree Fly—full-circle fly. This here is where we start setting our goals. Our goals are the final road map in fly. Girl, my wish is that you got smooth roads all the way through yo' journey.

We gonna' start at the hard place for many a fly chick—money. Money only part of the circle, though. Keep that in mind. Jest 'cause you can handle yo' money ain't mean you all-the-way fly.

120-Degree Fly—Money-wise Fly

Step One: Think on these things, girl. What do financial success mean to you? Is it havin' that big house on the hill like the Diva Turner? Or, would you prefer somethin' you can call yo' own an' fix up for the next few years. I ain't no financial wizard, but I do know that if you don't watch what you got, it's not gonna' sit there an' wait for yo' attention, girl. What you got will whoosh out the door, won't be seein' you no mo!

Cane Sense Project

- Go back over your dream map. Look at what you said you wanted to own. Make some decisions 'bout what's most important to you right now. What things do you want to work toward this year? Don't try to bite off more than you can chew, now. Pick the small stuff, the easy stuff. Pick the thing you know you have a chance of doin'. Make a list of those things you wantin' to work toward this year.

- Next, write down how much each item will cost. Check prices if you have to. (If you don't think you can ever afford to get it, then skip this, an' look at Step Two of Financially Fly.)

- Give yo'self a time line for reachin' the goal. I like to set quarter goals. There're four quarters in a year and it jest seem easier to break my dreams down that way. Might take you longer. If you want to take a trip to Hawaii, you might have to save up all year, I don't know. All I know is that this here where you gonna' need to employ discipline an' focus.

Mr. Thang's Guide to Fly

⚯ Once you got yo' goal and timeline set, figure out yo' plan to get there. Are you gonna' have to get up early to read a book on underwater basketweaving? Do you have to save twenty dollars outta' each paycheck to reach yo' goal? Know how you gonna' do what you want to do. Then, get to work. Keep yo' eyes set on that mountain an' don't let nothin' but a big thing take yo' focus off where you headin'. Once you deal with the big thing, get back on focus.

Step Two: Don't let nobody tell you that you got to have a college degree to make money, 'though a college degree help, 'specially if you a Black American. If you got it like that, then you ahead in the game an' you already know most of what I been sayin'. If you didn't, or don't, have the wherewithal to get you a degree—an' many folks don't—then you need to know how to educate yo'self so that you can move ahead career-wise, or start yo' own business.

Somethin' Out of Nothin'

A lot of folks say it take money to make money, but that ain't necessarily so. You develop yo'self an' yo' skills an' you can find the money you need to get yo' ideas off the ground. I said it befo', people pay cold, hard cash for skills. They pay cash for creativity an' good ideas, too.

What else you need to make somethin' outta' nothin'?

A i n e A. T h a n g

1. Education—regular schoolin' or self-schoolin'
2. Focus on gettin' to yo' goals

We done talked 'bout focus, an' most folks know how to get regular schoolin', so I'll just bend my attention to gettin' self-educated.

Self-education look like this:

Got educated—You decide what you want to spend yo' time, yo' life, yo' talent doin'. Then you take college classes, community classes, or a couple of hours each week at the local library an' educate yo'self on these things.

Gettin' educated—Ms. Fly don't stop once she in the know. Just like you update yo' wardrobe, update yo' knowledge. An' now, since you know all there is to know 'bout makin' them killer baskets underwater, then you got to educate yo'self on how to sell yo' wares. Educate yo'self on presentin' yo' products. You can find 'most ev'ry kind of information at the local library or bookstore. An' don't forget the internet. You can find just 'bout anythin' you want to know on the internet. 'Course, you still need to do a check out on what you find on the internet, make sure they tellin' the truth.

Continuin' education—There's no such thing as bein' done with gettin' an education. You think you know it all? Wait a year an' watch what you know get changed up, or wore out.

Ms. Thang's Guide to Fly

That's the thing 'bout this generation, ya'll can't just live with the way things always been. Ya'll a bunch of revolutionary sisters. That's awright, though. It's all good. Just don't stop puttin' into yo'self. An', please, don't spend yo' time puttin' a bunch of trash in yo' mind. You look at the rap world an' how people thinkin' they could bring destruction into other people's lives with they music find that destruction knockin' on they own door. Some brothers might playa hata on that Will Smith kid, but that's a brother got it goin' on. He a Spencer for sure. Man work hard an' ain't 'bout puttin' up walls betwixt Blacks an' Whites. Here's my point: Ms. Fly ain't got time to start fights over race. Ms. Fly ain't got time to gang bang an' talk hard trash. Ms. Fly ain't got time to be profilin' destruction. Ain't no Ms. Fly pointin' a condemnin' finger at folks who break through. She too busy makin' her way to the top.

Some in the 'hood might be keepin' it real like that, but I guess they ain't known real, if real is Black people dyin' by the hand of they own.

Rest in peace, Rod Marable.

Next bit of fly you want to get a handle on is physical fly. You get this handle an' you halfway there.

+120-Degrees of Fly—Body-wise Fly

Now, after all the talkin' I been doin' 'bout not bein' a hoochie, Ms. Fly know she got to take care of her outer appearance, too. Havin' it together body-wise mean bein' fit— not a bag of bones, but healthy. God didn't make ev'rybody to be a toothpick, an' bein' overweight is a call for health problems you don't need. Walk. That's all you got to do. Leave that TV behind an' walk. Or, pick up them Tae Bo tapes. I been seein' old, old women doin' Tae Bo. If they can, don't tell me Ms. Fly can't.

The other part of body-wise is to watch yo' mental health. Thinkin' negative can destroy you. Now, I ain't here to dog nobody, least of all rappers. Most rap music, good music. Some folk call it the poetry of the Black people. But Granny Fly got a problem with rap music that don't see no good in anythin' but gettin' with someone for a hot minute or two. Rappers, ain't got nothin' to say but how they killin' an' spillin', ain't keepin' it real. C'mon now. Killin', spillin', and keepin' ain't all that life 'bout. Now, I know my speakin' the gospel truth ain't 'bout to change what's sellin' on the streets, but I'm talkin' to Ms. Fly. Girl, don't be fillin' yo' mind with nothin' but negative. I ain't sayin' lie to yo'self, but spend some time focusin' on the positive.

I don't do what they callin' affirmations, but some people swear by 'em. All I know is that havin' a healthy mind require thinkin' on the positive side.

Positive: I know I can an' so I will move my life in a forward direction. Yes, there's times, lots of times in this nursin' home, that I think I can't. When I start to thinkin' I can't, then it's time for my MHB—Mental Health Break. (Maybe old fly girls need more MHB's than young ones.) Still, all fly divas need to have the right thinkin' 'bout life. That's what

Ms. Thang's Guide to Fly

keepin' mean.
 Keep it real, girl.

Ms. Thang's MHB:

Stop what you doin', if you can; if you can't, then do this at the end of the day befo' you go to bed.
 Think through yo' day. What was good? What could've been better? What gots to go? What steps will you take to change the bad? Folks is lazy these days. They're more willin' to accept the bad than to change the bad. Fly divas exchange the bad for good.
 Ms. Fly take time each day to reflect, to put somethin' good into her soul. You ain't comin' up with the goods if you ain't refillin' yo' soul. Refill with good music, good reads, good friends, good love, an' the like. Don't feed yo' soul no bad stuff. That's keepin' it real.

Awright. Granny Fly 'bout to take you there. I'm talkin' to the races, now. Since you a spirit, girl, ain't no true fly without takin' care of the other part of you. Yo' spiritual self.

+120-Degrees of Fly—Spirit-wise/Relationship-wise Fly

Somehow, Americans done become a nation of people don't want a God. We think we too advanced, too smart, too above the idea of God. A lot of folks feel they God, so maybe that's the problem—a real higher power get in the way. Now, there's a lot of Black folks still holdin' on to believin' in God, more so than any other race in America. I figure that sets us up for a blessin' or two—hope you ain't blockin' yourn. By now ya'll know Ms. Thang been sittin' up under some preachin'. Now, I believe there's a Supreme Creator but, even if I didn't, I still believe in the idea of one.

Why should a fly girl bring spirit-wise to how she think 'bout herself?

Spirit-wise equal fly in a lot of ways. What can believin' in a Creator do for Ms. Fly?

- Believin' in a Supreme Creator help you accept that you ain't no accident. You a gift to the world from the Creator.

- Believin' in a Supreme Creator help you accept that the people 'round you made in the Creator's image. They need love. They need respect. An' they need to be held accountable for they actions of destruction against others made by the Creator.

- Believin' in a Supreme Creator help you follow the Creator's command to love yo'self an' treat yo'self with respect. You deserve respect from yo'self.

- Believin' in a Supreme Creator help you create. You create an' recreate yo'self. You create healthy, lovin' relationships. You create from the wealth within.

Ms. Thang's Guide to Fly

Without believin' in a Supreme Creator, we got a tendency to be selfish, don't care 'bout nobody but ourself. Believin' in the Creator change yo' actions, 'cause, if you really believe, would you put drugs in yo' body, which the Creator call a temple? What 'bout sex? Would you use another person for yo' own selfish pleasure?

I hope not.

Get yo'self some spirit-wise goals, girl, cause faith is fly.

CANE SENSE:

Now, since I'm so close to Glory, I got fierce reason to believe. That's all fine an' good, but just 'cause I'm old don't mean I got to believe. They just as many old people don't believe in a Creator as they is young peoples.

Some think Faith is a crutch for the weak-minded. Maybe it is, but a crutch got a purpose to help you walk when you can't do it on yo' own. Truth be known, some of them people callin' faith a crutch, the same ones abusin' drugs, alcohol, sex, an' theyselves. They usin' crutches that kill an' destroy. Fact is, they can't hang when the goin' gets rough, like it sometimes do in life. They profilin' tough, but it ain't real.

Look here, ain't no shame in usin' a crutch when you need it. The shame is in pretendin' you stronger an' better than other folk. The shame is in placin' yo'self above others 'cause they do believe.

One other thing: Avoid people usin' yo' fly faith to try and trick you. The Creator warned us to be careful of them usin' faith to get rich. Just 'cause you believe in a Creator don't mean you s'posed to check them brain cells He gave you at the door to the church house, givin' all yo' money to some charlatan. What you s'posed to do is think on yo' own. Check the preacher out. Know what you believe an' why. Seem to me that a lot of times the Creator get the blame for our own bad choices.

Add it up, Girl!

$$\begin{array}{r} 120\text{-Degrees of Money-wise Fly} \\ +120\text{-Degrees of Body-wise Fly} \\ +120\text{-Degrees of Spirit-wise Fly} \\ \hline 360 \text{ degrees (full-circle) Fly!} \end{array}$$

Ms. Thang Speaks

The Nature of Fly

CHAPTER 11

▼

The Nature of Fly

You got folks came befo' you; folks who walked the hard path, clearin' out what they could for the ones who would come after.

Somehow, fly come to mean the way you present yo' outside self to the world. That's only part of the circle. Ms. Thang is here to testify 'bout the nature of fly. To keep it real, I got to be honest. The way some of these young people actin' these days, makes me wonder what in the world I was thinkin' when I let my children do sit-ins an' march for freedom. Freedom for what? For our boys an' girls to make music videos 'bout killin' each other an' "doin' it doggy style"? For our people to disrespect Black leaders like Colin Powell 'cause he not "Black enough"? (He Black enough to go back to the neighborhood an' help our young people rise out of hard circumstances.)

Now, I ain't tryin' to call nobody out they name, but if you want to understand the truth 'bout bein' fly, you got to understand the truth 'bout Black history, 'cause Black folk invented fly. If you don't understand that, how you goin' to make choices 'bout creatin' yo' future an' yo' legacy?

Aine A. Thang

Back in Africa, folks used to worship they ancestors. I ain't askin' nobody to light a candle an' pray to me after I done passed over, but take a minute to think 'bout where you come from. Ain't no stork dropped you from the Heavens. You got ancestors.

You got folks came befo' you, folks walked the hard path, clearin' out what they could for the ones who would come after. Ms. Oprah Winfrey said it this way, "For ev'ryone of us that succeeds, it's because there's somebody there to show you the way out."

That somebody can be one of yo' ancestors, a granny, a mother, a sister, somebody from yo' own blood. Or if you ain't got a lot of respect for yo' blood, then decide who you do got respect for an' adopt them, take they heritage as yo' own.

Yo' ancestors ain't got to be yo' blood. If Shaq can say biological didn't bother, then the rest of us can say it, too. We'll stand behind him if folks start actin' crazy.

Take a minute to think 'bout yo' ancestors—blood-kin or adopted. If they blood-kin, write they names down. You owe these ancestors of yourn. You think you got rough times? Please, on the news they talkin' 'bout how there mo' black middle class than ever befo'. 8-G free, you ain't seen hard times. Slavery was 10-times harder than times is now, an' we survived.

Jim Crow was 20-times harder than times is now, an' we survived.

Yo' ancestors survived an' brought they dreams forward to this generation, to you.

Ms. Thang's Guide to Fly

Don't let yo'self down, 'cause when you do, you lettin' yo' ancestors down.

Don't look on that as pressure, 8-G, look on it as motivatin'. When times get hard, take yo' mind off of yo'self, and think 'bout the folks that came befo' you in the struggle.

Somehow, someway, they made it through, so can you.

Maybe you ain't got a lot of respect for yo' parents an' grandparents; maybe they ain't done nuthin' for you but bring you into the world. But that, at least, gave you a chance to create a life for yo'self. You ain't got to repeat nobody else's mistakes. You ain't got to be downtrodden, under nobody's feet. You can make yo' own choices. You can choose yo' own path. Befo' you start, though, you got to remember the past.

This here the seventh an' eighth generation of freedom, for people of color, for women. We a blessed generation. An' folks always sayin' how freedom ain't guaranteed. Never was a truer word spoken. I been through some stuff in this country, seen things go from bad to worse and then to good. What I know is that freedom an' safety an' power ain't never guaranteed to nobody. You got to fight for 'em—always. You got to keep fightin' for 'em. An' when you got 'em, respect 'em. Be responsible with 'em.

Lot of folks wanna' blame the Creator when bad things happen. Hmph! Now, that's how you use the Creator for a crutch, blame ev'rythin' on Him.

God don't create problems in yo' life, he use problems in yo' life to help you. Recall what the Word say, now, "All things work together for the good. . . ." An' the Lord's prayer talkin'

A ine A. Thang

'bout "deliver us from evil."

Last I heard only terrorists harmed innocent folk. Hurtin' the innocent ain't God's business, it's man's.

Freedom always come with responsibilities. Lot of folks think freedom mean doin' whatever you want to do. Even I wish that was true, but it ain't.

That's hoochie thinkin'.

It ain't freedom. Seems to me the message of freedom to this generation been goin' somethin' like this:

Take yo' clothes off.
Talk nasty as you want to.
Be nasty as you want to be.
Become the Supreme Hoochie.

Only way of makin' it is sellin' drugs, doin' drugs, gang-bangin', hatin' Blacks who are educated an' successful ('cause they wouldn't be successful if they hadn't crossed over).

Well, you tell Ms. Thang, 8-G Free, where those kind of freedoms takin' you? Where yo' legacy? Yo' Shirley Chilsolms? Yo' Martin Luther King, Jrs.? Yo' Barbara Jordans? Yo' Maia Angelous?

What 'bout supportin' people out there tryin' to make it to that kinda free?

Seem to me, when somebody get a little bit of success, somebody else steady tryin' to knock her down.

Mick ears, girl, yo' sister-girl got a right to live uptown. She ain't got to come livin' in yo' neighborhood to keep it real.

Folks preachin' that noise need to clean up they neighborhoods, if they want success to come payin' a call.

Stop pointin' a condemnin' finger at folks who break through. Ain't nobody got time for excuses.

The Color of Responsibility

We all better recognize that even though, as a people, we all different, we heirs to a legacy of helpin' one another where we can. Sometime that legacy can be a burden, but ain't nobody make it without a helpin' hand. If you find a sister that got spark, help her nurture it. Help her grow it. You fly enough for that, ain't you?

An' last, what 'bout my generation? Do you know how hard we fought for you to be able to live free—truly free? Do you know how many of us fought, an' died, an' was denied so that you could have yo' fly life? Don't you fly divas owe us somethin', too? Somethin' like R-E-S-P-E-C-T?

An' if you can't do that, at least be responsible with the legacy so that we don't go back to what was.

Seem like those of us paid the highest price ain't gettin' no rest. Instead, we been sentenced to watchin' our legacy die from crack cocaine, or gettin' shot for a few dollar bills. Our legacy is gettin' diseased an' havin' all kinds of tribulation 'cause of ignorance. Our daughters an' granddaughters been told that the only way to get success is to give up they self-respect.

That ain't right. It ain't right. An' I ain't seen nobody

sayin' nothin' against right. Well, I got my legacy in this generation, an' I ain't 'bout to go to the hereafter without leavin' some good word for those that comin' after me. I'm lookin' to the future, to my granbabies future. I ain't had no choice but to speak out an' hope this word plants some good seed.

If you ain't understood what Ms. Fly had to say, let me put it together for you one mo' time: True fly is 'bout becomin' who the Creator meant you to be. True fly is 'bout sharin' yo' gift, yo' life, yo' spark, yo' fire with the world.

Fly ain't one-dimensional, it's a circle, 360-Degrees. It ain't jest the outside package. It's the inside, too. When you fly, you got it goin' on money-wise, body-wise, and spirit-wise. You deal with the issues tryin' to hold you back; and you push and push and push 'til you on the mountain. Once you there, baby girl, you shout yo' fly anthem from the top of that mountain.

Then you go back down the mountain. Get somebody to bring up with you now that you know the way. Teach yo' mountaintop song to yo' sister.

Get the words, right, girl. Ain't nobody ever say we shall undercome. It's we shall overcome, an' overcome, an' overcome, an' keep overcomin' 'til at last, Glory overcome us.

That's it.
That's all.
That's fly.

In peace,
Ms. Thang.

Ms. Thang's Guide to Fly

I belong to the club because I finished the book.
I started the dream. I'm living my life.

Ms. Fly

Date:

If you need a reminder of where you headed in life, cut out the card above and keep it with you. Ain't got to show it to nobody, this card for yo' eyes only.

Don't fill it out unless you read the book and mapped yo' dream, otherwise, you falsi-fly.

Know the code.
Original Fly Code: Believe, Reach, Achieve, Become, Teach

Appendix

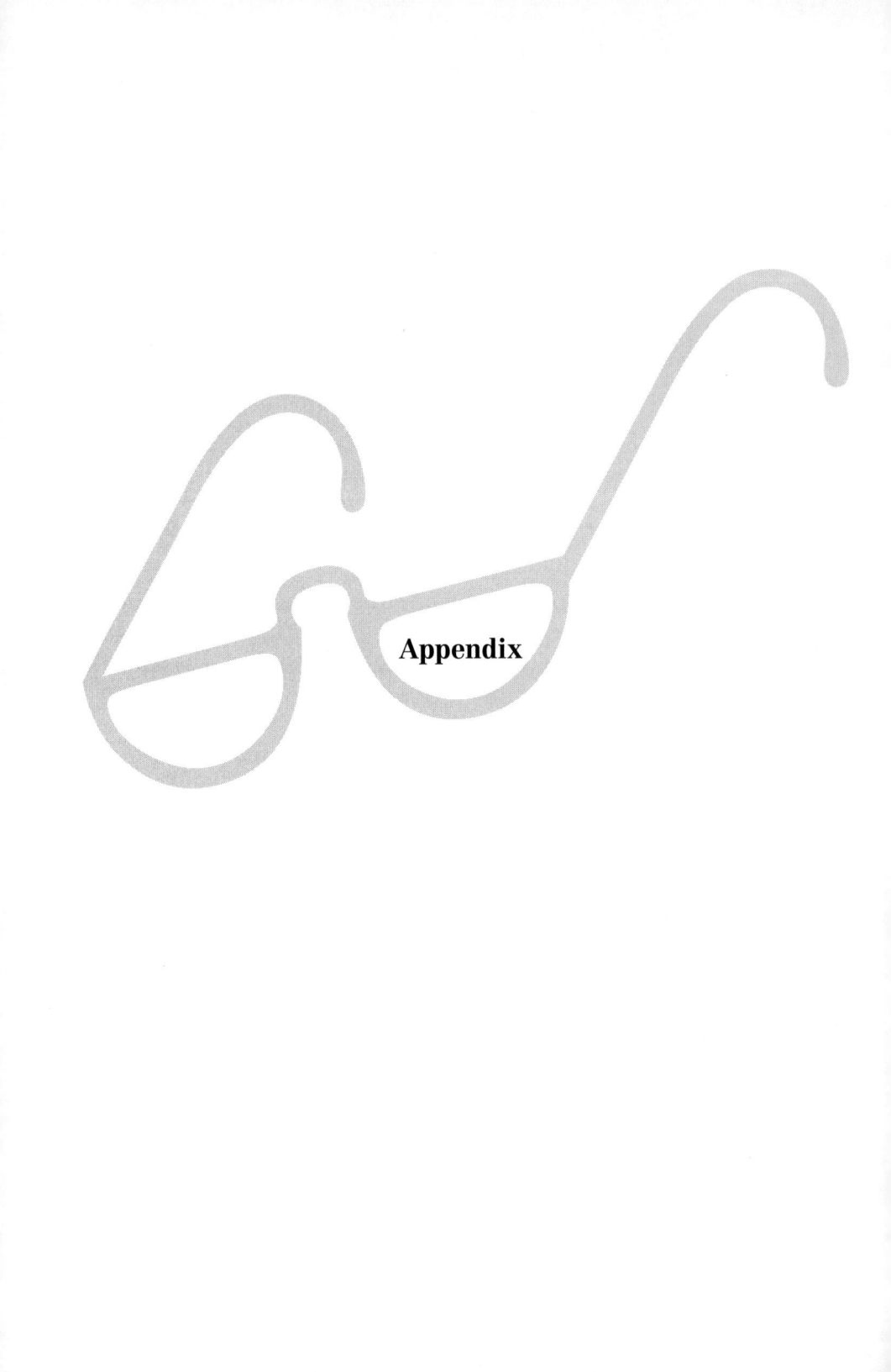

Ms. Thang Terminology Guide

1-D = One dimensional, a body got the looks, but no intelligence

8-G Free = Eighth Generation of Free people (both Black and White 'cause slavery affected everyone)

A to Z = From beginning to end.

Ann = or Miss Ann, White woman

As God is my secret judge = As God is my witness

B-of-A Busta = A loser with a college degree, also a B-of-S busta

Baby Girl = What you call yo' girl, usually said by an older female to a younger one

Better ask somebody = When sister-girl acting like she know something, but she don't. That girl better ask somebody

Better recognize = Recognize, realize

Be 'bout = Doing something meaningful.

BGT = Black Grandma Talking (play on BMT—Black Man Talking

Blessed = A believer, or Christian

Blow up = To do well career-wise, or money-wise

Boojee = To act uppity, or arrogant

Break you off something = To give you the best I got

Brang the noise = To tell the truth, loudly

Buck wild = Someone acting crazy

Busta = A Loser

Cane Sense = Good sense, or common sense that comes from being whipped upside yo' head with Ms. Thang's cane

Call myself = Trying for a goal, but not reaching it

Can't kill nothin', won't nothin' die = To have a hard time.

Changes = Problems in yo' life

Check yo'self = Monitor your actions

Chillas = Young women, girls

Chitlins = Pig intenstines, considered good eatin' in the South

Color Scale = Gradation of skin color from light to dark

Color struck = An African American obessessed with, and preferring light-complexioned Blacks and/or Whites; a negative term

Come correct = To talk with some good sense

Community = African Americans as a group. Community of women

Crazy = Going against what you ought to be doin'

Creep = To sneak out with somebody other than your spouse or partner

Dap = Respect

DBI = Declaration of Black inferiority, a Black person who feels inferior to people of other races

Deliver = To perform something to the maximum

Dipped = Dressed well

Dippin' = Stickin' your nose into other people's business or conversation

Dis = To discount or show disrespect to someone

Don't play = To be serious, determined

Dog "nobody" out = To criticize.

Drama = A situation of emotional distress, turmoil, or conflict

Drop = To enlighten; to inform; to explain

Drop Knowledge = To enlighten; convey knowledge

Falsi-fly = Fake fly, not the real deal

Fass = Promiscuous-acting woman, sleep with anybody

Fass-track hoochie = Woman on the hoochie career track

Five-and-dime = Poorly dressed; showing bad taste in clothes

Five-and-dime glory = Fifteen minutes of fame

Flava = Attractiveness, style

fly-losopher = A body that study fly

Frog = A fass person who hops an' jumps into anybody's bed

Froggy = Someone who wants to start a fight

From the get-go = From the beginning

G'd up = Dressed up, according to whatever one's standards are, also moneyed up

Ghetto-fabu = Ghetto-fabulous. Dressed in ghetto threads, but stylin' anyway.

God don't like ugly = "God don't like bad behavior

Good to go = Ready to participate

Grown = Used to describe a young person who is acting an'/or looking like an adult; used in a negative sense

Grown folk = People who act like they s'posed to act: responsible, sensible, mature

Grown folks' business = adult matters

Golden shower = When someone does you wrong

Hard-headed = Refusin' to listen to reason

Hoochie = Girl who act fass and nasty; promiscuous; also called "Hoochie Mama" or "Hooch"

Hoo-rah = A lot of noise, loud talk

Hound = a man who will sleep with anyone

IBWC = Intelligent Black Womens Coalition

IFWC = Intelligent Fly Woman's Club

In the day = In the past

In the street = Not at home; Rippin' and running around town

Issues = Challenges or problems

Mackin' = Flirting

Macaroni = older term for "mack daddy"

Mess = Nonsense

Mick ears = Listen closely, with ears as large as Mickey Mouse

Mickey Ears = See above

No count = Not important

O-fly = original fly

One mo once = One more time

Original Fly Club = Also known as O-Fly Club

Original Fly Code = Believe, Reach, Achieve, Become, Teach

POC scale = (People-of-Color scale) The varied gradients of color in the Community

Playa = A player; someone who's just out for hisself

Play somebody = Deceive someone

Profile = Presenting yourself in a certain manner

Rags = Stylish clothes

Raise up = To leave

Recruiting = On the look out for an attractive person

Run the Street = Out partying, not at home

Run wild = To act crazy; to not listen to reason or good sense

Sadditty = Uppity

Salty = Angry

Serve = To provide sexual favors

Shoot the gift = Use the gift of gab

Show an' prove = To speak well; To prove your point conclusively

Skills = Talents and abilities (Talents are natural, inborn; abilities can be taught.)

Smooth = Stylish

Spencer = A good man

Sponsor = Someone who takes care of a woman in return for favors; a sugar daddy

Springtime hoochie = A old hoochie holdin' on to youth

Stay in the Street = Never at home, always out

Steady = Something that is done frequently

Talk that talk = Speak in a convincing manner

Talk crazy right = Don't allow yo'self to dwell on the ngeativ. If you gonna act crazy, then do it right. Help yo'self out with yo' craziness

Whilin' = Hanging out, spending time

Wrong Side of Crazy = This is the type of crazy that will cause you to end up holdin' yo'self back

Ms. Fly Reading List

Boyd, Herb. *Autobiography of a People.* New York: Anchor Books, 2000

Buckingham, Marcus, and Clifton, Donald O. *Now, Discover Your Strengths.* New York: The Free Press, 2001

Bunkley, Anita R. *Steppin' out with Attitude: Sister Sell Your Dream!* New York: Harper Collins Publisher, 1998.

Capodagli, Bill, and Jackson, Lynn. *The Disney Way.* New York: McGraw-Hill, 1999

Carr-Ruffino, Norma. *The Innovative Woman.* Franklin Lakes, N.J.: Career Press, 2001.

Sterling, Dorothy, editor. *We Are Your Sisters: Black Women in the Nineteenth Century.* New York: W.W. Norton, 1997.

Also Available from Yeva Press

Winter Skin
> A provocative collection of poetry that invokes winter as a lens through which to view life as a person of color.

Girl Gifts
> This wonderful gift book for young girls and preteens blends the pictures of Master Photographer Kirk Duit with a rhyme by author F.M. Avey

Gateway
> Patrick Scott is accused of a crime he did not commit. With nowhere to turn for help, Patrick must depend on Demetria Jensen in a game where every path leads to lies and danger.

And from *Cadeau Moments* romance:

Deeply
> Sterling Matheson fights to protect his family from Palomita Santanello, a woman he believes to be a blackmailer. When he meets Jewel Turnquist, Palomita's beautiful attorney, can he defend both his family name and his heart?

A Lifetime Loving You

Cory Miller has rocks for brains. There's no other explanation for his behavior. First he asks his best friend Nance to help him win the girl of his dreams, then he decides that it's Nance he really wants.

To learn more, visit our website at: www.yeva.com